THE COMING AGE OF ACCELERATED LEARNING

Developing Better Individuals, Communities, and Organisations While Getting Ready for the Future

By Ali Kursun

First published by sparkChief & Co. in 2017

© Copyright 2017 sparkChief & Co.

All rights reserved. No part of this publication may be reproduced, stored in retrieval system or transmitted, in any form or by any means, electronic, photocopying, recording, or otherwise, without the written prior permission of the author.

Note to Librarians: A cataloguing record for this book is available from Swiss National Library (NL) in Switzerland at http://www.helveticat.ch/search/query?theme=Helveticat

ISBN: 978-1545558638

sparkChief Publishing

This book was published on-demand in cooperation with sparkChief & Co. Publishing. On-demand publishing is a unique process and service of making a book available for retail sale to the public taking advantage of on-demand manufacturing and internet marketing. On-demand publishing includes promotions, retail sales, manufacturing, order fulfilment, accounting and collecting royalties on behalf of the author.

For international book sales:

sparkChief & Co. Publishing
25 Route de Lullier
1254 Jussy, Geneva, SWITZERLAND
phone +41 22 346 24 05; email to bookorders@sparkchief.com

Order online at:

www.sparkchief.com/services_book.html
Also available on amazon.com, blurb.com and other online book sellers.

To my parents, who provided me with the opportunity to be who I am, to my wife who supported me to be who I am, and to my kids and their future …

TABLE OF CONTENTS

INTRODUCTION		9
CHAPTER 1:	THE KEY PROBLEM FACING SOCIETY TODAY – AND TOMORROW	16
CHAPTER 2:	THE HIDDEN COSTS OF SELF-IGNORANCE	31
CHAPTER 3:	POTENTIAL BARRIERS TO SUCCESS – AND WHY WE SHOULD BOTHER	45
CHAPTER 4:	TECHNOLOGY AND THE ROAD TO SELF-KNOWLEDGE	61
CHAPTER 5:	GETTING READY FOR THE FUTURE: THE ROADMAP	77
CHAPTER 6:	PRACTICAL STRATEGIES FOR FOLLOWING THE ROADMAP	95
CHAPTER 7:	PRACTICAL EXAMPLES OF SELF-ASSESSMENT USERS	101
CONCLUSION AND FUTURE THOUGHTS		111
REFERENCES		121
INDEX		123

ACKNOWLEDGEMENT

My thanks are due to many and various people. Two individuals, who, in particular, inspired me and sparked the idea for this work so many years ago are: Daniel Pink, with his book, "A Whole New Mind: Moving from the Information Age to the Conceptual Age" and Keith Ferrazzi, with his book, "Never Eat Alone: And Other Secrets to Success, One Relationship at a Time.

Those who directly supported me with the research described here and especially Virginia (Ginny) McMorrow, my editor, who was so amazing in the way she directed me and helped me to develop my manuscript.

Many friends, clients, colleagues, and relatives contributed to this book, and, in particular, I need to thank all those who participated in my interviews over the last 12 years. Finally, my thanks to all who have invited me to speak to them and who remind me that this work really does make a difference.

Many thanks to you all!

INTRODUCTION

Throughout my life and consulting career, I have encountered thousands of people who struggled with the decision about what to do in life. Although this phenomenon is prevalent across a wide range of age groups – from age 15 to 60 – I have also met with older people who struggled with that same difficult question. In more than 20 years of personal and professional endeavour with thousands of daily interactions with diverse people across the globe, I have observed this universal question cut across age, race, religion, culture, and traditional group.

My obsession with this question is personal. I believe I have an obligation to share my thoughts and perspectives in order to do justice to my conscience.

The answers to that question are as different as the individuals: People may be following their destiny or the road prescribed by conventional wisdom. Others look to role models, inspired by their stories or, perhaps, their own family's legacy and dreams. Some people pick one criterion to lead them, for example, their passion, believing that if they work hard enough, they will achieve anything they want in life. Then there are others who passively wait for someone else to discover their talents and skills and finally realise their dreams for them.

Many individuals consider their path in a haphazard manner, often resulting in deep unhappiness. They attempt various endeavours, failing to realise any satisfactory outcome. In fact, unhappy people become and remain unproductive and inefficient, seldom succeeding in any effort in the long run. With so many dissatisfied, discontent individuals, society at large pays a huge cost, as the family, community, corporations, and nations feel the adverse effects.

Very few people are willing to investigate this hidden cost and help others move beyond their trouble. In today's world, the concept of helping others is typically associated with benevolent work – not necessarily guiding others in their search for answers. Consider the trend for corporate initiatives around "social responsibility." This short-term thinking says, "let's have a fancy social responsibility programme so that we look like we are doing good for the community in which we live, but not necessarily engage in resolving the root cause of these problems." Even some very focused medical research initiatives, for example, throw money at specific problems, but do not build awareness around changing the habits that cause most of these conditions.

The Need for Clarity and Direction

To answer the complex question – "what do I do in life?" – one needs a deep understanding of how personal fulfilment is realised. Although there are as many "fulfilment" paths as there are lives on this planet, it does not mean that we should stop striving to shed light on this issue. We all play a key role in finding the solution, whether we are individuals, educators, or employers.

My conviction about this issue is simple: The biggest killer of all time, ignorance, still persists and underlies the majority of problems we face in life. In my view, the true definition of ignorance is "not wanting to learn," which has caused the death of millions and wiped out civilizations. "Not wanting to know" is at the core of individual problems, as well.

For example, so many people do not want to learn about their capabilities. Or, perhaps, their consequential context misguides them, as their environment – be it family situation, employer, neighbourhood, or even religious, ethnic, or social community – holds sway and determines their fate. When events or incidents affect their lives, such people nod and believe that it is their lot in life. In either situation, they fail to maximise their potential to live a fulfilling life. Ignorance or "not wanting to learn" causes pain in people's lives, with devastating implications that result in tangible or intangible loss. It also has an enormous impact on the way we live, work, communicate, and generate value in our society.

Unfortunately, this killer disease continues to spread around the world at full speed, parallel to the advances in our cognitive capabilities and intelligence. Many people forget that everything is relative. What we were able to create, develop, and enhance in terms of intelligence over the last century and during the first decade of this century is behind us. What happened yesterday no longer dictates what will happen tomorrow.

Going forward into the foreseeable future – the only way to succeed –

we must recognise other critical factors that significantly impact our personal lives:

- The amount of information to which we are exposed every new day grows exponentially. Yet, our ability to learn is either idle or at most linear. Are we so overwhelmed that our minds and intellect cannot absorb more data, particularly if we can no longer decipher what is truth? How can we overcome this inability?
- The scope of knowledge in any field is transforming into a more complex contextual understanding. Without acknowledging that everything, ultimately, is connected, how can we envision the whole picture? How will we be able to identify the impact of our actions (and lack of action) on our families, communities, colleagues, and organisations?
- Current education systems are becoming obsolete much faster than we can comprehend. People perceive learning as a cumbersome activity and time-consuming effort due to lack of up-to-date and up-to-speed learning tools. If educators do not stay abreast of the rapid pace of change, how can they provide a strong foundation for students entering the world at large and the marketplace? Where is the initiative and drive to create the requisite tools?
- We increasingly put our trust in the hands of technology, hoping that technology alone will bring solutions to our problems. If technology fails us – and possibly alienate us

further from ourselves and others – are we prepared to handle that eventuality?

The Need for Self-Awareness

There is an urgent need to learn faster and understand as much as possible even deeper than we do today. Everything around us is speeding up except our learning process. To be fulfilled, we require an accelerated learning process.

The prerequisite for that accelerated learning is to urgently learn about ourselves. Society should gear all education systems toward that aim. The deeper we learn and understand our inner lives, the faster will be the acceleration and the better our understanding about the world around us. The most relevant content is that within ourselves. Only when we comprehend what makes us tick as individuals will we be able to successfully address the intelligence within our realm and achieve better living conditions, relationships, communities, and, ultimately, fulfilling lives. How can we even entertain the thought of being intelligent in our world if we do not have a glimpse of our inner selves?

There is little time to think and decide. We need to act. Technological changes are rapidly transforming the way we interact with the world; change happens very "suddenly." A word with many attributes, "suddenly" involves the concepts of "surprise" and "newness" and "uncontrollable." Suddenness represents and breeds change, provoking immediate action and cultivating authenticity.

We must continuously remind ourselves that knowledge is our currency and understanding is power. We need to act on our understanding of ourselves to design a roadmap that leads out of "not knowing" and eradicates ignorance – starting from within ourselves – to create better futures for ourselves and all others.

The Roadmap to Satisfy Those Needs

The following chapters provide a roadmap to the first and fundamental step of discovering one's self and starting the journey to answer the question, "what do I do in life?" This step-by-step guide can help diagnose where you stand vis-à-vis your personal development and point to actions you can take to achieve fulfilment. Bear in mind, however, that it is not a one-size-fit-all solution book. Personal discovery and progress requires many hours, days, and, sometimes, years of reflection and alignment. The suggested framework is simply a model that requires personal customisation and homework, conducted both in isolation and with feedback from trusted advisors.

This book contains the following topics:

- Chapter 1 explains why it is important in both the present and future to begin the journey with discovering yourself.
- Chapter 2 discusses the importance of accelerated learning and its impact on us as individuals as we navigate through the 21st century.
- Chapter 3 presents potential barriers to success in our efforts and emphasises the reasons to overcome these difficulties.

- Chapter 4 illustrates how technology can support our path to self-awareness.
- Chapter 5 outlines the roadmap involved in a new algorithm to help users achieve self-knowledge.
- Chapter 6 provides practical strategies to follow the suggested roadmap.
- Chapter 7 offers practical examples of how different groups can use the self-assessment tool.
- The Conclusion presents thoughts for the future and necessary steps we need to take.

CHAPTER 1:

THE KEY PROBLEM FACING SOCIETY TODAY – AND TOMORROW

The increasing importance of learning has created an unprecedented demand for different and higher forms of understanding, awareness, and leadership. The intersection of new technologies and exponential growth of knowledge accumulation will accelerate this demand during the 21th century and beyond.

The life span of knowledge and human skills today is shorter than ever, increasing the pressure on individuals to remain at the forefront of any domain throughout one's career or a lifetime. In the midst of continuous human development, progress, and technological revolution, university degrees represent just the beginning of a life-long continuing education process. Although some people may view "life-long learning" as merely a slogan or buzz word, it is quickly becoming a crucial factor in our evolution as individuals, educators, and employers.

Looking back, the resources of the material-based economy were oil, coal, and steel. In contrast, for the present and future, the resources of the new economy are creativity and the ability to effectively acquire, deliver, process, and synthesise ever-increasing knowledge. Those individuals who are effectively trained, educated (either self-taught or through academic institutions), and well-informed will be able to endure and prosper. Unfortunately, those who lack this foundation will become economically and socially obsolete.

As a consequence, learning has become even more critical for both individuals and organisations of all types and sizes in all industries around the world. In today's competitive sphere, a four-year degree is barely a prerequisite to participating in the industries of the future. Although life-long learning is a requirement for existence and longevity, gaining a firm foundation in undergraduate programmes can support the long-term journey.

Ensuring That Students Have What They Need

The National Survey of Student Engagement (NSSE)[1] explored so-called "high impact practices," or HIPs, in undergraduate institutions. Due to the positive effects on student learning and retention, special opportunities – such as learning communities, service-learning, research with faculty members, study abroad, internships, and culminating senior experiences – make up these practices, which share common traits.

---

[1] National Survey of Student Engagement, Research Brief #1 (May 2013).

They:

- Demand considerable time and effort.

- Provide learning opportunities outside the classroom.

- Require meaningful interactions with faculty and other students.

- Encourage interaction with diverse others.

- Provide frequent and meaningful feedback.

For students to achieve optimal experiences, the NSSE holds that educational institutions need to accomplish the following:

- Provide opportunities for participation in at least two HIPs during the course of the undergraduate programme: one in the first year, and one later that is related to the student's major.

- Ensure that all students have such opportunities, examine whether some majors are less likely to participate, and observe to what extent first-generation students take advantage of HIPs.

- Reduce barriers to participation and encourage all students to recognise the potential for their involvement.

- Ensure that programmes are high quality and show evidence of their effectiveness.

- Know how students benefit from their experiences.

HIPs offer promising results. But how successful are educational programmes in general when it comes to guiding and preparing students for the future? A study[2] that compared the perception by employers and students provided an interesting and somewhat disheartening difference when asked about the preparedness of recent graduates. Since employers are the ones who accept or reject job applications, it would appear that students need to reassess the practical value of their skill base.

Category	Employers (%)	Students (%)
Working with others in teams	37	64
Staying current on technologies	37	46
Ethical judgment and decision making	30	62
Locating, organising, and evaluating information	29	64
Oral communications	28	62
Working with numbers and statistics	28	55
Written communication	27	65
Critical and analytical thinking	26	66
Being innovative and creative	25	57

---

[2] Hart and Associates, "Falling Short? College Learning and Career Success" (2015).

Another study[3] considered different undergraduate majors and the students' confidence in their education and future outlook. Arts majors (67.1%) and humanities majors (66.4%), followed by communications majors (64.2%), reported the highest percentages of having "very much" confidence in their creative thinking and problem-solving skills. On the other hand, only 12.1% of arts majors reported having "very much" confidence in financial and business management skills. It would seem that any major – whether scientific, business-oriented, or in the arts – should focus on balancing courses of study to provide students with a strong base from which to launch their careers.

Focusing on the Most Critical Questions

Students, however, are not the only group in need of direction. Almost everyone at some point is looking for help in answering questions that are broadly similar. The questions refer to a universal need to go forward and seek advancement – and, ultimately, search for happiness:

- Students wonder which subject to study in college and, therefore, ensure future employment.

- Employees and job seekers desire to know how they can progress in their career and earn more pay and better benefits.

- Employers need to know how to attract and retain winning teams to remain viable players in the marketplace.

---

[3] Amber D. Dumford and Angie L. Miller, "But What Are You Going to Do with Your Life? Arts Majors, Future Plans, and Career Skills," presentation, National Association for Gifted Children (2016).

- Governments seek to know how to improve the competitiveness of their nation.

On an annual basis, in order to answer these questions; students spend US$6.3 trillion[4]; employees and job seekers spend US$10 billion[5]; employers spend US$292 billion[6], and governments spend 5.1% of their gross domestic product (GDP).[7] And yet:

- The majority of students do not know which subject to study at college, yet invest heavily and without any deliberation in higher education (meanwhile, building a future with huge debt that hurts their financial progress).

---

[4] Source: http://www.gilfuseducationgroup.com/education-market-factbook. The market for global education expenditures by 2017, according to estimates, includes e-learning, edu-gaming, social/learning communities, test preparation, language, and others, ranging from early education and K-12 through to post-secondary, higher education, and corporate learning.

[5] Marketdata Enterprises, US Market for Self-Improvement Products and Services (December 2012). In 2012, Americans spent this amount on self-improvement books, CDs, seminars, coaching and stress-management programs; latest forecast: 6.1% annual growth in 2012 through 2016.

[6] Doug Harward, "How Big is the Training Market?"(Trainingindustry.com, June 6, 2014). According to the global market for training expenditures in 2013, North America represents about 46% of the global market (US$141.7 billion), Europe is about 29% (US$89 billion), Asia is 10% (US$31 billion), India is 7% (US$21.5 billion), Australia is 3% (US$9.2 billion), South America is 2% (US$6.3 billion), Africa is 1% (US$3.6 billion), and the rest of the world is 1.1% (US$4.6 billion). Approximately 75% of the global expenditure on training is in North America and Europe. Asia and India, the two most-populated regions, combined make up about 17% of the global market. Source: Trainingindustry.com.

[7] Organisation for Economic Co-operation and Development, Education at a Glance (2011). Average spending by (OECD) countries as a percentage of their GDP on educational institutions at primary, secondary, and tertiary levels is about US$8,300 per student. In 2008, this figure represented 6.1% of the collective GDP. The amount exceeded 7% in Chile, Denmark, Iceland, Israel, Korea, Norway, and the US.

- The majority of employees are not happy with their jobs but still hope that things will change one day in the future.

- The majority of employers have difficulty in recruiting the right people needed to sustain good performance, but invest heavily in training for the wrong skill sets for the wrong employees while wasting valuable organisational resources.

- The majority of governments waste scarce public resources to finance "mass-produced" education systems that are out-dated and impersonal, but expect their nations to thrive in the future.

Unfortunately, there are too many solutions providing disparate answers that are insufficiently strategic and comprehensive to capture the full picture. Off-the-shelf help, advice from friends and relatives, unfocused training, and conventional wisdom appear to be common – and often, unsuccessful – remedies. So wherein do we find the answers?

The Importance – and Lack – of Personal Leadership

The definition of leadership in modern origination has evolved over the last 20 years, becoming very exclusive rather than inclusive. Merriam-Webster's traditional meaning is "a position as a leader of a group, organisation, etc. ... the power or ability to lead other people." In line with that definition:

- 91% of respondents to the Millennial Leadership Study[8] aspire to be a leader.
- Almost half of the millennials queried define leadership as "empowering others to succeed."
- 43% said their biggest motivator to be a leader was to empower others.

These noble sentiments, however, miss a critical point. Every person is, or should be, his or her own leader – whether a student, educator, employee, business executive, or government official. Believing that only a few qualified people have the right to be a leader is inherently incorrect. To be a responsible family member, community member, citizen, educator, employee, colleague, business manager, or executive, every individual must be a personal leader. If they are not, how can people claim to lead others? Understanding that one should not seek leadership in others – but in oneself – is the starting point to truly strive toward having a better family, community, society, organisation, corporation, and nation.

Should the status quo change with a new definition of leadership, consider the tremendous responsibility it would place on the shoulders of parents, community leaders, educators, government officials, corporate shareholders, and executives. Nevertheless, this key transformation should be a top priority. If ignored, weak leadership in any endeavor has the potential to rapidly consume our natural, human, and financial resources.

---

[8] Conducted by WorkplaceTrends.com and Virtuali (July 21, 2015).

This reinvented definition is urgent, vital, and the most important ingredient to achieving fulfillment and success in our personal lives, communities, societies, and organisations. Every passing day is lost to mediocracy, unhappiness, inefficiency, conflict, untapped human effort, wasted resources, and underperforming organisations. Without individuals accepting the challenge to take the lead on a personal level, no sustainable solution exists to our diverse difficulties.

The Problem with the Status Quo

Companies around the globe are experiencing a growing talent gap at the executive level. According to the Global Workforce Leadership Survey,[9] 46% of respondents said that leadership was the most difficult skill to find in their workforce. In fact, only one-third (36%) listed leadership as an existing skill in their organisations.

An analysis of responses by U.S. businesses and HR leaders to a global study[10] showed a critical need to improve leadership development initiatives. Although U.S. respondents made up nearly one-third of the 7,500 global respondents, their answers generally mirrored responses from other world regions. "The best thought-out business strategy will fail miserably if the leaders within an organisation don't have the skills to make it come to fruition," said Dennis Baltzley, senior client partner and global head of leadership development solutions for Korn Ferry Hay Group. The study found that only:

---

[9] Conducted by Saba and WorkplaceTrends.com (March 31, 2015).
[10] Conducted by the Hay Group division of Korn Ferry (2016).

- 17% were confident they have the right leadership capabilities in place to execute on strategy.

- 18% were confident that their leadership team demonstrated the behaviors needed to successfully deliver on strategic business priorities.

Such studies point to the problem with today's status quo. Unfortunately, the majority of people have defaulted to average performance in many aspects of their lives, not just work. At the very best, people appear to be content with mediocre activity and results in every plan they put forward. We convince each other that if our peers are in similar circumstances, then that should be the norm. After all, how could we even think of doing better? And why should we bother?

Our understanding of outperformance has shaped into some sort of magic. We seek only science in the tangible world and call the intangible world an art form that is difficult to measure. We shy away from the unknown without bothering to explore what is possible. Because of this lack of personal leadership – combined with our acceptance of average outcomes – the problems and difficulties we face continue to accumulate. This approach, or thinking by default, breeds mediocracy.

Over the last 20 years, this backward thinking has prevailed as we become content with our future, encouraging the emergence of disengaged family members, community members, students, educators, citizens, employees, and executives. The conclusion? Nobody cares.

This dangerous thinking carries an enormous price tag, a cost hidden from corporate or government income statements and balance sheets.

The Root Cause of the Problem

In a nutshell, the root cause of the status quo comes down to these factors: our misconceived incentive philosophy combined with weak leadership bred by this misalignment in our families, communities, schools, organisations, and governments.

The most critical question every CEO needs to ask – regardless of whether the person leads an organisation, a government agency, a community association, a family, or one's individual life – is how do we want our incentive philosophy to work? Incentive philosophy is not about how an organisation rewards its members. Rather, it is about knowing how people should work and cooperate to achieve a shared outcome. If leaders do not deeply understand why and how people work within an organised structure, then they can do anything they want, yet still not achieve optimal performance and results. This point holds true whether in choosing the right course of study, career move, hiring, or serving the public.

Optimal performance is about maximum return, whether financial, personal, or societal. Maximum return is not about what peers or the market holds that one can achieve – for example, 3% to 5% annual growth for a business endeavor (although with today's norms, these numbers are considered great) or beating peers or the market by another 3% or 5% -- which is a mediocre thought. Maximum return is about significant outperformance, about multiples, never a small percentage differential.

To achieve optimal results, it is clear that people who are motivated and engaged in their own and the group's welfare have a strong connection to the overall productivity, profitability, effectiveness, and viability as a player in the appropriate market. According to a recent survey[11] of companies, only 32% of employees are engaged at work, with 50.8% not engaged. In fact, engagement statistics have been flat for the past 15 years. These appalling statistics indicate a misalignment throughout the corporate world brought about by misalignment of incentives. What use are incentives if they do not work? Companies that outperform significantly better align their incentive philosophy than those that perform or underperform – an amazingly efficient approach to outperformance.

There appears to be more to outperformance than simply offering rewards to deserving individuals, although rewards remain a very important tool to support motivation to achieve results. That said, however, it is long past time for managers (or educators or individuals) to resist using their favorite medicine to solve difficult problems: the "reward pill."

> *"We are all crazy about the reward pill and use it like Aspirin."*

Companies dole out this particular medication as pharmacists distribute Aspirin for various ills, including headache, stomachache, and blood

---

[11] Gallup, The State of the American Workplace (2017).

thinning. In organisational terms, the reward pill seeks to resolve promotion, retention, and hiring issues. For educators, it strives to address lack of student engagement. And for individuals, it attempts to reclaim the lost and misguided mindset. But remember, in neither health care nor other care, the pill is not a cure; it only eliminates the symptoms. In fact, one should not even need to take a pill if the root cause of the problem is effectively addressed.

The Gap Between Personal and Organisational Goals

The truth behind underperformance and misalignment of incentives/rewards lies in the misalignment of personal and organisational goals. If one is not clear about one's personal goals in life, it becomes difficult to discuss shared goals between an individual and the organisation to which the person belongs. Thus, we needlessly consume resources (personal or corporate) when individuals choose the wrong educational path, work for the wrong organisation, hire the wrong person to achieve a set of specific objectives for the organisation, or misdirect government resources.

For educators, student admissions can become a nightmare of weeding out individuals uncertain of where they want to go or be in life. Further, these young people are often busy applying to the wrong institution for the wrong course of study.

From the employer's perspective, mountains of applications from unqualified candidates overwhelm business managers and HR staff, waste time and money, and often lead to bad decisions. The search for hidden talent, particularly in leadership positions, can uncover the leaders – the individuals who lead themselves, as well as possess the capability to lead others – through the use of technology that can match individuals' skills and desires and vision with what an organisation really wants and needs to go boldly into the future.

What has become the norm of mediocre outcomes and outlooks no longer serves all stakeholders (shareholders, students, educators, parents, employees, employers, governments, and other partners we work with to generate value). While it benefits an exclusive few individuals who have become professional experts who think of value creation only as a personal endeavor to lead others, CEOs in any capacity should not allow this breed to prosper at the cost of all other stakeholders. Shareholders and boards should make CEOs accountable for hiring only the leaders who share this new vision of the future organisation. It is only then that we will have a chance to change and improve – by finding and cultivating talented individuals who can take charge of their own growth while empowering others to achieve shared goals.

The Storm and Its Aftermath

Complacency prevails. To change the interpretation of leadership to effectively nurture the right individuals requires open-mindedness and courage. Rarely do people happily accept change, and this new thinking will be transformational, arriving like an unwelcome storm. But after the winds die down and the sun reappears, we will rebuild as we always do, relying on the human need to move forward.

The result will be worthwhile. Organisations will survive longer and succeed far better than those of prior years, which have often faded into oblivion. And individuals will be more successful in their ability to lead fulfilling personal and career lives, while encouraging others to join in a united effort to better themselves and the organisations with which they interact. Built within the underlying foundation are life-long learning, deep self-awareness, and personal leadership. With these elements in place, the results may prove to be outstanding.

CHAPTER 2:

THE HIDDEN COSTS OF SELF-IGNORANCE

While some individuals and entities are content to move along at a mediocre, uninspiring pace, the hidden cost of failed self-knowledge and the prevalence of complacency in all aspects of modern life have an adverse impact on our limited resources. Individuals and organisations often waste time and money on misguided student education and mismatched employee recruiting. Finding a solution to minimise such inefficiency is critical for individuals to achieve a brighter future and organisations to flourish. The first step toward this goal is understanding the factors that encourage waste, followed by implementation of technology that can lead to optimal harmonising of personal and organisational desires.

Educational Repercussions on the Family Budget

Families, and often the students themselves, go into heavy debt to pay for college and university degrees that may or may not result in a successful career. In light of the expense, more than 70% of full-time students receive grant aid to help pay for college.[12]

These costs can quickly add up, according to an article in thespruce.com.[13] Even before the student is accepted into an institution, the college application process in the US, for example, can be financially painful. The pre-attendance price frequently includes the following fees:

- College counseling can cost US$160-US$300 an hour; US$3,000-US$5,000 for a two-year package (counseling, essay help, and application know-how); or a flat US$500-US$1,000 to help students choose schools that would be a good fit in terms of abilities and interests.

- Requisite examinations, estimated at about US$60 each, add up as the typical college applicant takes some exams more than once. Test preparation courses – depending on whether it is an online course, a multi-week class, or a private tutor – can range from several hundred to several thousand US dollars.

- College visits, tours, and interviews can add US$200 to US$5,000 to the family budget, depending on the location of the college.

- College application fees range from US$30-US$80 per application.

---

[12] The College Board, Trends in College Pricing (2016).
[13] Jackie Burrell, "The High Cost of College Applications" (November 20, 2016).

And these fees are payable before the student actually goes to class, when the family (or student) faces the actual cost of tuition and housing. According to a study,[14] between 2004–2005 and 2014–2015, these prices rose 33% at public institutions and 26% at private nonprofit institutions. In contrast, the price at private for-profit institutions decreased 18%.

Comparing 2015-2016 and 2016-2017, the College Board[15] reported the following year-on-year increases of average published tuition and fees:

Category	2015-2016 tuition and fees	2016-2017 tuition and fees	Increase (before adjusting for inflation)	Average tuition, fee, and room and board
In-state, public four-year sector	US$9,420	US$9,650	US$230 (2.4%)	US$35,370
Out-of-state, public four-year institutions	US$24,070	US$24,930	US$860 (3.6%)	US$35,370
Private nonprofit four-year institutions	US$32,330	US$33,480	US$1,150 (3.6%)	US$45,370
In-district public two-year colleges	US$3,440	US$3,520	US$80 (2.3%),	N/A
Full-time students in the for-profit sector	US$15,660	US$16,000	US$340 (2.2%)	N/A

---

[14] US Department of Education, National Center for Education Statistics (2016), Digest of Education Statistics, 2015 (NCES 2016-014).
[15] The College Board, Trends in College Pricing (2016).

Institutions also charge fees for services, such as the library, campus transportation, student government, and athletic facilities. In addition, tuition can vary by major, with students in the sciences, engineering, computing, pre-medicine, and fine arts often paying more. This fact adds to the financial impact if the student changes majors once – or, even, a few times.

According to an article on choosing majors,[16] this decision should be intentional, based on knowledge of one's self. When the wrong choice is made, the implications can be harsh. In reality, the author holds, all students are likely underprepared when choosing a major: An estimated 20% to 50% of students enter college as "undecided," and an estimated 75% change their major at least once before graduation.

The article cited a survey in the College Student Journal that asked students about their career decision-making process. Factors included a general interest the student had in the subject; family and peer influence; and assumptions about introductory courses, potential job descriptions, and characteristics of the major. The answers implied that students made their choices based on influence and assumption, rather than through an understanding of their own personal goals and values.

Due to the potential positive or negative impact the choice of major can have on the overall student experience, the author holds that it is

---

[16] Liz Freedman, Penn State Division of Undergraduate Studies, The Mentor Journal, "The Developmental Disconnect in Choosing a Major: Why Institutions Should Prohibit Choice until Second Year" (June 28, 2013).

imperative for institutions to delay major selection until the second year, when students are more developmentally ready and educationally prepared to make an effective choice. Ultimately, a student who makes a more informed decision in the second year, based on personal goals and values, will engage more in the college experience and be more successful academically, personally, and professionally.

The Cost of Education Debt Is a Global Problem

The implications for educational choices and costs are not merely a problem in the US. An article in US News and World Report[17] cited the following points:

- American student loan debt has ballooned to more than US$1 trillion, with more than 7 million borrowers in default, according to reports by the Consumer Financial Protection Bureau. Although college students in other countries take on student loans, the level of debt incurred by student borrowers in the US is unmatched abroad.

- Although tuition is free at public universities in Argentina, Iceland, Norway, and Sweden, zero tuition does not equal zero student debt. In 2012, approximately 900,000 Swedish students received help from the government totaling close to nearly US$3.5 billion, to cover fees and living expenses.

---

[17] Kelsey Sheehy, US News and World Report.com, "Undergrads Around the World Face Student Loan Debt" (November 13, 2013).

- In Japan, an estimated US$5 billion in student loans were past due in 2011, according to the Japan Daily Press.

- Tuition in the UK is more on par with that in the US. Students in the UK can borrow loans for tuition and living expenses from the government-run Student Loans Company. Approximately 958,000 students did so for the 2011-2012 school year, according to the company annual report.

When it comes to attainment of post-secondary degree for those in the age 25-34 group, the US has one of the least cost-effective post-secondary educational systems among developed countries.

Country	Post-secondary spending as share of gross domestic product (%)	Post-secondary attainment, age 25-34 (%)
Finland	1.9	39
Norway	1.4	47
Korea	2.6	65
Spain	1.3	39
Sweden	1.8	42
Australia	1.6	44
Switzerland	1.3	40
Ireland	1.6	48
Belgium	1.5	44
Israel	1.6	44
Canada	2.5	56
France	1.5	43
Poland	1.5	37
Netherlands	1.7	41
Italy	1.0	20
United Kingdom	1.3	46
Germany	1.3	26
United States	2.6	42
Portugal	1.4	25
Austria	1.4	21

Source: Georgetown University Center on Education and the Workforce, analysis of data from the Organisation for Economic Cooperation and Development (2010).

The Graduate Unemployment Factor

In light of the expenditures faced by parents and students, the College Board[18] report pointed out an important fact. When students take longer than two years to earn an associate degree or more than four years to earn a bachelor's degree, there are financial implications for the future, whereby students forgo earnings from reduced participation in the labor force. Consider:

- The more quickly students earn their degrees, the more time they have to earn college-level wages and reap the financial benefits of post-secondary education. According to the US Census Bureau,[19] bachelor's degree recipients between age 25 and 34 had median earnings that were 69% (US$18,876) higher than those with high school diplomas in 2015.

- However, according to a 2013 study,[20] many young adults experience a delay in the "on-ramp" from education to full-time career and family formation. The age at which young adults reach the median wage level has jumped from 26 to 30. Making the move to a decent job is difficult for many millennials, who represent 40% of the unemployed population in the US.[21] This group faces higher tuition and student loan

---

[18] The College Board, Trends in College Pricing (2016).
[19] US Census Bureau, 2015 Income Data, Table PINC-03.
[20] Anthony P. Carnevale, Andrew R. Hanson, and Artem Gulish, "Failure to Launch," Georgetown University Center on Education and the Workforce (September 2013).
[21] Anthony Carnevale, Georgetown University Center on Education and the Workforce, cited in an article in Newsweek, "Millennial College Graduates: Young, Educated, Jobless," by Leah McGrath Goodman (May 27, 2015).

debt, as well as stiffer competition for employment. Part of the problem is the perceived gap between education and job readiness.

Another factor involves the expectation of life-long learning and a continuous upgrading of skills necessary to adapt to new workplace technologies, both trends that have replaced the traditional on-the-job learning process. In the 2013 study,[22] the author holds that organisations should consider streamlining curricula to promote college affordability, degree completion, and acquisition of competencies that have labour market value for employers.

A two-year study[23] discussed the so-called skills gap and what managers desire in an employee. When considering a composite "ideal," the employers in the study envisioned "a hard-working individual with appropriate technical training (knowledge as well as the ability to apply technical information), solid problem-solving skills, and the abilities to communicate well, work in teams, and to continually learn new things." The competencies they desire are not discrete skills but part of a larger whole that comprise "a person's habits of thinking, behaving, and problem-solving."

---

[22] Anthony P. Carnevale, Andrew R. Hanson, and Artem Gulish, "Failure to Launch," Georgetown University Center on Education and the Workforce (September 2013).
[23] Matthew T. Hora, "Beyond the Skills Gap," National Association of Colleges and Employers Journal (February 2017).

HR Repercussions on the Corporate Budget

Once students advance to the labor market, the problem shifts to employers. The corporate world spends billions of dollars and countless hours every year to recruit qualified employees, despite sometimes-disappointing success rates not only in hiring but also retaining key staff. According to a research study,[24] US companies spend nearly three times the amount on recruiting efforts than they do on training per employee. The most mature recruiting organisations – defined as those considered strategic enablers of the business – spend US$6,465 per employee, on average, compared with only US$3,258 among organisations at the lowest level of maturity with reactive, tactical recruiting. But, according to the research, the investment is worth it: High-impact organisations have 40% lower new-hire turnover and can fill vacancies 20% faster.

With regards to timing, another study[25] offered a different perspective. Candidates who rejected an offer pointed the finger at employer mistakes: Companies do not streamline their hiring practices to prevent their best candidates accepting another offer. Such companies also do not fully understand the target candidates' most important priorities – a disconnect between personal and organisational goals – thereby losing them to the competition. The report cited the time for extending job offers as three to six weeks from the candidate's first interview, a shift from one to four weeks reported in the second half of 2015.

---

[24] Bersin by Deloitte, Talent Acquisition Factbook 2015: Benchmarks and Trends in Spending, Staffing, and Key Recruiting Metrics (April 23, 2015).
[25] MRINetwork Recruiter and Employer Sentiment Study (2016).

The Additional Burden of Mis-Hires

According to an article[26] on employment costs, the four most common reasons for hiring mistakes include the following:

- Hiring decisions are at least 80% made as "gut feeling" or "based on appearances."

- Scarcity and/or urgency mindset involves a belief that few candidates have the necessary skills or the recruiter is driven by outside pressures to fill the spot immediately and settle for mediocre candidates.

- The hiring manager is dazzled by first impressions, how good the person looks on paper, credentials, advanced degrees, and well-prepared interview responses.

- There is a lack of understanding about the difference between and/or having the necessary tools to discern top talent (based on qualifications) vs. best fit talent (perhaps a better fit with respect to organisational culture, and so on, not just having appropriate skills).

A costly hiring mistake - the cost of a "mis-hire" – is the unconscious avoidance, denial and/or toleration of underperforming employees. The higher the level of the position, the quicker the cost of a mis-hire

[26] Denise Corcoran, Empowered Business.com, "Shocking Costs of Hiring Mistakes" (October 30, 2013).

increases exponentially. The article cites Brad Smart, Founder, Topgrading, Inc., regarding the potential cost for a mis-hire:

- 14 times salary for employees earning a base salary under US$100,000.

- 28 times salary for employees earning US$100,000 to US$250,000.

Besides the typical direct and indirect costs of dealing with finding new employees (such as recruiting, interviewing, reference checking, lost productivity in beginning months, and so on), employers need to consider long-term opportunity costs: substandard service; lowered employee morale and substandard performance in other employees; missed deadlines; customer dissatisfaction with product quality, customer service and/or lost trust/faith in the company; and missed sales opportunities.

Overwhelmed by mountains of candidate submissions from unqualified people, as well as internal pressure to fill job vacancies, the result is not surprising: Time is wasted, money is ill spent, and fallible decisions are made. This archaic process almost guarantees that people "who know people" are the only candidates being hired – whether or not the applicant is a good fit. Company policies that compensate for employee referrals encourage this outcome. Although employee references may (and, hopefully, should) prove advantageous, the risk of presenting individuals with the wrong skills and experience can lead to potential trouble down the road if the referral does not work out to the manager's expectations.

In a typical situation, the hiring process drags on for weeks, sometimes months. As the employer follows the traditional recruiting method, some negative repercussions are possible:

- Time spent in preparing the job search, writing advertisements, conducting candidate interviews, evaluating meeting results, making and negotiating offers, and filling out paperwork

- Money wasted on advertisements, agency fees, external posting websites, new hire sign-on bonuses (if turnover is high), and relocating key candidates (if necessary)

- Management dissatisfaction with loss of productivity, inefficient output, and decline in potential business and company performance when a job is vacant too long or another employee (unfamiliar with the job responsibilities and unhappy with an added workload) is temporarily filling in

- Unqualified applicants responding to advertisements and overwhelming hard-pressed (and too few) HR staff who may make subjective judgment calls simply to fill another vacancy

- Displeased shareholders (and customers) if the overall performance of the company falls off

Lower Costs Are a Necessity

As a society, we must each contribute to reducing the hidden costs of self-ignorance and struggle against complacency and mediocrity. By guiding young people in their search for education and a career, as well as adults seeking meaningful employment, our efforts can significantly cut back the waste in time and money. But the endeavor is not for the weak in spirit, as it will require time, intelligence, persistence, commitment – and the right vehicles.

CHAPTER 3:

POTENTIAL BARRIERS TO SUCCESS – AND WHY WE SHOULD BOTHER

It would be naïve not to consider the barriers to success when implementing any new approach to develop leadership, accountability, and self-awareness in order to boost the success of – and align – our personal and organisational efforts. Therefore, it makes sense to identify these potential barriers as potential hurdles and then develop strategies to mitigate the risks involved. These new approaches not only involve making things right, but also showcasing that there is indeed a better way to succeed and that we want the best for every stakeholder without exception. Among the potential barriers are the following factors.

Shareholder Philosophy
I do not know of any explicit shareholder philosophy based on mediocre performance expectations, as the main reason people invest in a business is to obtain maximum returns on their invested capital.

Further, I am not aware of any explicit shareholder approach that wishes ill on other stakeholders and focuses instead solely on personal financial outcomes.

Investors (people) like to talk about their investments and the choices they make in terms of growing their capital. In the majority of cases, especially in publicly traded and family controlled investments, investors, without exception, seek new ways to increase profits and improve margins. They keep a close eye on how management executes their investment strategy.

However, shareholders are not always well-informed, particularly when it comes to large organisations. Although the purpose of the board and management team is to safeguard the interests of investors, by law (in a majority of jurisdictions), shareholders also expect them to respect certain operational ethics. On the surface, there should not be any suspension of intentional resistance to new approaches from the shareholders' perspective – that is, shareholders cannot explicitly intend to exploit the workforce for their own gains without honouring the right of each employee to achieve self-knowledge and fulfil the individual's potential.

Yet, on the other hand, explicit intentions sometimes may not be authentic; although legally justified, they implicitly drive the purpose of a given investment to satisfy only shareholders' gains. Whether or not this type of implicit intention is agreed or even articulated behind closed doors is another matter for investigation beyond the scope of this book. However, if suspension is perceived, there is very little potential for the executive team to attempt new approaches that would jeopardise shareholders' current investment philosophy.

Current Leadership and Management Intentions

If current shareholders have explicit and implicit intentions to consider all other stakeholders' interests along with their own to maximise returns for all stakeholders, management's key focus need only be guarding the interest of all stakeholders. Management's role in delivering returns while safeguarding the interest of all stakeholders should link to management's ability to be as transparent as possible. With management under constant scrutiny by the board, having a specific mandate from shareholders to manage the operations of their investment with optimum efficiency, it is common sense for the organisation's leadership to continuously seek productivity gains. By explicit default, the expectation for the management team is that they serve all stakeholders (shareholders, management, employees, clients, suppliers, and so on) and fulfil their accountability by facilitating a value generation for all.

The only problem with such facilitation is that, as an orchestrator, while aiming to safeguard the interest of all stakeholders, management might attempt to benefit more than other stakeholders. I do not know of any explicit intentional desire by any management team to achieve personal gains (although there have been disappointments in certain organisations, I prefer to assume that these are exceptions); however, if there is any implicit desire for personal gains, such people, in my opinion, belong in prison rather than on management teams. Legal means should address implicitly-driven leadership or management teams who only guard their own interests. In essence, management should support innovative approaches to maximise returns for all stakeholders.

Existing Employee Population Disposition

The key purpose of any employee in working for any type of organisation is to generate value for all stakeholders. Although the definition of value may differ by entity, the key purpose remains the same. No employee should explicitly seek only personal gain. Fortunately, legal implications and internal management policies exist to address such acts. However, as some employees may have implicit intentions, at the very least, an organisation that recognises such patterns of behaviour should discharge such employees.

Although many reasons can explain why some employees focus on generating value only for their own gains, the typical rationalisation is that they are encouraged to do so or live in a working environment that implicitly allows such behaviour. Obviously, other personally driven reasons may exist due to individual inclinations. However, the fact remains that such employees will resist transparency and will misguide others around them, causing frustration throughout the organisation. Management needs to identify such individuals as early as possible to avoid their preventing the company from deploying new approaches.

Political Environment in which One Lives

If one's country has an unstable political environment or discourages freedom of expression, it becomes challenging to advocate self-discovery and awareness. Some governments thrive solely on that promise, not wanting citizens to be more self-aware or to excel due to their knowledge of personal capabilities. Organisations established in these markets face the same problems.

Current Educational Systems

Unfortunately, many current education systems are archaic and based on an outdated economic model. There has been no large-scale transformational change in either developed or emerging markets regarding education. Learning still involves delivery of specific content and methods that are, unfortunately, not suited to every individual. Education does not provide adequate options for many students and lacks personalisation, representing a considerable barrier to preparing the younger generation for the future and facilitating their personal progress.

There is an urgency to alter and improve education systems in almost every country. If there is no action to modify these systems to address the needs of today's generation, schools will continue to produce unhappy and frustrated individuals in society. Self-discovery and awareness should be at the core of future system transformations.

Reasons to Push Through the Barriers – For Individuals

In light of the struggle and hurdles to make changes to move forward, it may seem easier to accept the status quo and settle for a life and career of mediocrity. But isn't that a waste of one's potential for happiness and success?

Abraham Maslow's concept of self-actualisation and the psychological hierarchy of needs speaks of fulfillment and meaning in life. According to an article in Psychology Today,[27] Maslow contends that self-actualisers are highly creative, psychologically robust individuals.

Maslow's Hierarchy

> 1. Physiological needs, such as needs for food, sleep and air
>
> 2. Safety, or the needs for security and protection, especially those that emerge from social or political instability
>
> 3. Belonging and love including, the needs of deficiency and selfish taking instead of giving, and unselfish love that is based upon growth rather than deficiency
>
> 4. Needs for self-esteem, self-respect, and healthy, positive feelings derived from admiration
>
> 5. And "being" needs concerning creative self-growth, engendered from fulfillment of potential and meaning in life

The article explains that Maslow identified self-actualising people as "individuals who are highly creative, who have peak experiences, and who are able to resolve the dichotomies inherent in opposite contraries such as those constituted by 'freedom and determinism,' 'the conscious

---

[27] Ann Olson Psy.D., "The Theory of Self-Actualization, Psychology Today online (August 13, 2013).

and the unconscious,' as well as 'intentionality and a lack of intentionality'."

Self-actualisation, self-fulfillment, self-awareness, happiness – whatever one considers to be an optimal state – has benefits that impact all aspects not only of one's own life, but also those with whom we interact, be it our family, co-workers, friends, and the community at large. An online Twitter chat, cited in "How Happiness Affects Your Health,"[28] provided the following comments and ideas from participants:

- Happiness indicators include life satisfaction, health, and community and civic engagement.

- Happiness is hard to measure, but easy to recognise.

- Having creative and purposeful work to do is a key factor in happiness, but balancing work and personal obligations is important.

- Once basic needs like food and housing are met, higher incomes do little to boost happiness. Ultimately, people find value in their connections with others. Having support through friends, family, and social networks reliably predicts happiness.

---

[28] Dr. Anjuli Srivastava, ABC News via Good Morning America, Twitter chat hosted by Dr. Richard Besser of medical experts (March 27, 2013)

- People who meditate have an improved sense of calm and wellness. People who express religious or spiritual faith also report being happier.

- Expressing gratitude fosters happiness. Performing acts of kindness or altruism boosts moods.

- Happiness is contagious.

Self-awareness and personal empowerment should be an individual's priority, as they form the foundation from which we can move forward on the path to making life-affirming decisions.

Reasons to Push Through the Barriers – For Employers

Employers – and other organisational entities – have a strong motivation to ensure that their employees have the opportunities to advance along their personal development path. In the end, employee growth can only serve to support the company's strategic goals – as long as they are compatible. In a recent article of the Gallup Business Journal,[29] Gallup's research showed that companies with engaged workforces have higher earnings per share (EPS) and recovered from the 2008 recession at a faster rate. Businesses with a critical mass of engaged employees outperformed their competition.

---

[29] Susan Sorenson, Gallup Business Journal, "Employee Engagement Drives Growth"(June 20,2013).

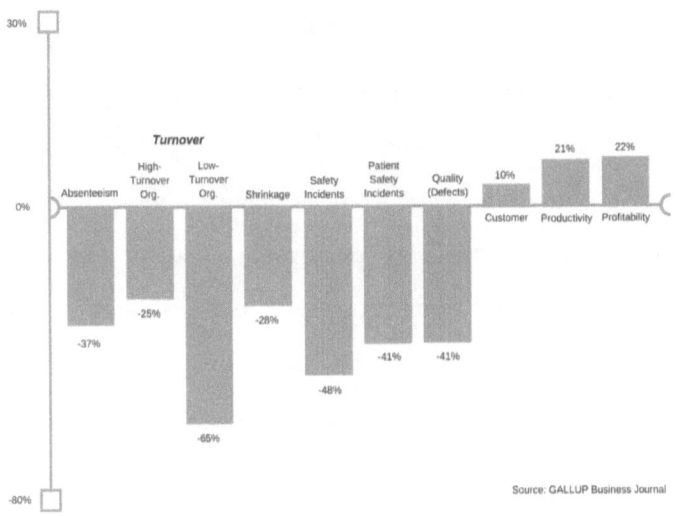

Source: Gallup Business Journal

According to the State of the American Workplace report[30]:

"Organizations have nowhere to hide. They have to adapt to the needs of the modern workforce, or they will find themselves struggling to attract and keep great employees and therefore customers….. The one thing leaders cannot do is nothing. They cannot wait for trends to pass them by, and they cannot wait for millennials to get older and start behaving like baby boomers. …"

"Organizations falter in creating a culture of engagement when they solely approach engagement as an exercise in making their employees feel happy. It is true that engaged employees, which Gallup often describes as enthusiastic, energetic and positive, feel better about their

---

[30] Gallup, The State of the American Workplace (2017).

work and workplace. However, engagement is not determined by an abstract feeling. Happiness is a great starting point, but just measuring workers' satisfaction or happiness levels and catering to their wants often fail to achieve the underlying goal of employee engagement: improved business outcomes. Organizations have more success with engagement and improve business performance when they treat employees as stakeholders of their future and the company's future. They put the focus on concrete performance management activities, such as clarifying work expectations, getting people what they need to do their work, providing development and promoting positive coworker relationships."

The Gallup research provided statistics to illustrate the advantages for progressive employers willing to offer employees the opportunities to further their personal development and become engaged in their commitment to the company According to the research, engaged employees:

- Make it a point to show up to work and do more work — highly engaged business units realise a 41% reduction in absenteeism and a 17% increase in productivity.

- Are more likely to stay with their employers. In high-turnover organisations, highly engaged business units achieve 24% lower turnover. In low-turnover organisations, the gains are even more dramatic: Highly engaged business units achieve 59% lower turnover.

- Care more about the products and services they deliver to customers and the overall performance of their organisation. Highly engaged business units experience a 28% reduction in shrinkage (the dollar amount of unaccounted-for lost merchandise) and a 40% reduction in quality defects.

- Are more mindful of their surroundings. They are aware of safety procedures and diligent about keeping their coworkers and customers protected. Highly engaged business units realise a 70% decrease in employee safety incidents and a 58% decrease in patient safety incidents.

- Consistently show up to work and have a greater commitment to quality and safety. Understandably, these employees also help their organisations improve customer relationships and obtain impressive organic growth. Highly engaged business units achieve a 10% increase in customer metrics and a 20% increase in sales.

- Are more present and productive; they are more attuned to the needs of customers; and they are more observant of processes, standards and systems. When taken together, the behaviors of highly engaged business units result in 21% greater profitability.

---

[31] J. Helliwell, R. Layard, and J. Sachs, World Happiness Report 2017, NY: Sustainable Development Solutions Network (chapter on "Happiness at Work" by Jan-Emmanuel de Neve and George Ward).

Metrics such as these should be a wake-up call for complacent employers, who may think that salary is enough to keep employees engaged. However, research included in the 2017 World Happiness Report[31] found that although well-paying jobs are conducive to happiness, it is not the whole story. Some of the most important job factors that drove subjective well-being included work-life balance, autonomy, variety, job security, social capital, and health and safety risks.

Reasons to Push Through the Barriers – For the World at Large

The Organisation for Economic Co-operation and Development (OECD) Guidelines on Measuring of Subjective Well-being [32] define and recommend the following measures of subjective well-being: "Good mental states, including all of the various evaluations, positive and negative, that people make of their lives and the affective reactions of people to their experiences. … This definition of subjective well-being encompasses three elements:

1. Life evaluation—a reflective assessment on a person's life or some specific aspect of it.

---

[32] J. Helliwell, R. Layard, and J. Sachs, World Happiness Report 2017, NY: Sustainable Development Solutions Network (chapter on "The Social Foundations of World Happiness," John F. Helliwell, Haifang Huang, and Shun Wang)

2. Affect—a person's feelings or emotional states, typically measured with reference to a particular point in time.

3. Eudaimonia—a sense of meaning and purpose in life, or good psychological functioning.

Well-being is multidimensional, covering aspects of life ranging from civic engagement to housing, from household income to work-life balance, and from skills to health status, according to a report by the OECD.[33] The latest evidence on well-being indicates, predictably, that countries ranking in the top third of the OECD in gross domestic product (GDP) per capita terms tend to do well overall, especially in relation to material well-being outcomes such as household income and earnings. Nonetheless, countries can have comparative weaknesses in areas such as job security, air quality, housing affordability, and work-life balance at any level of GDP per capita. Other findings include the following:

- Different groups within a country's population can have very different well-being experiences. For example, the bottom 60% of the distribution owns 20% or more of total net wealth in the Slovak Republic, Greece and Spain, but less than 8% in Germany, the Netherlands, Austria and the US.

---

[33] Organisation for Economic Co-operation and Development (OECD), "How's Life? 2015: Measuring Well-Being."

- Better-educated people tend to live longer, but at the age of 30, tertiary-educated men can expect to live anything from four to 18 years longer than their primary-educated neighbors, depending on the country.

- In Italy, Belgium, Hungary, Australia, Luxembourg, and the UK, the long-term unemployment rate among younger workers (aged 15-24) is at least twice the rate among those of prime working age.

- As well as having low levels of income inequality, Nordic countries tend to have much smaller differences in quality of life outcomes – including gender and age-related differences.

- Not all children are getting the best possible start in life. Across OECD countries, one child in seven lives in poverty, almost 10% of children live in jobless households, and one in 10 report being bullied in school.

- There are striking inequalities in child well-being associated with family socio-economic background: Children from better-off families have better health, higher skills, higher civic engagement, and better relationships with parents and peers. Students from more advantaged families are also less likely to be bullied and more likely to feel a sense of belonging in school.

At present, some countries consistently harbor higher well-being than others. The World Happiness Report studied well-being in a number of countries, with the top 10 remaining the same when compared to the 2016 update, although some countries shifted their ranking. For 2017, the top 10, which are all small- or medium-sized industrial countries, are as follows:

1. Norway
2. Denmark
3. Iceland
4. Switzerland
5. Finland
6. Netherlands
7. Canada
8. New Zealand
9. Australia
10. Sweden

When one considers the conditions in various world regions, how can complacency and the status quo remain as is? By supporting the need for individuals to go beyond their existing situation to reach their potential, neighborhoods, countries, and world regions all stand to benefit.

Barriers Are Not Insurmountable

Acknowledging the genuine hurdles faced on both an individual and organisational level, the human condition strives upward and forward. Cooperation among people and organisations – whether community or job or government-related – can address the issues, given time, resources, and the right tools. In this day and age, technology is one of those tools that can support the path to empowerment, leadership, and self-awareness.

CHAPTER 4:

TECHNOLOGY AND THE ROAD TO SELF-KNOWLEDGE

Let's face it, the truth is simple and very easy to understand. If two people are compatible and complement each other's personalities, they will enjoy interacting with each other – whether socially hanging out or joining in a cooperative community effort or other endeavour – for a long time. The same concept is no different between employees/job applicants and employers. Unfortunately, the most significant trouble between employers and employees is that organisations do not take the time to assess that compatibility with an eye for truth or honesty – thereby resulting in a significant waste of financial and human resources.

The traditional view of "organisation" has changed from representing an entity based on a shared common vision, created to generate value for all its members, not just a select few. In this view, people tended to remain with the company for a long period, often thinking of the company as a "family" to which they owed loyalty and that, in turn, took care of its family members.

Consider the viewpoint of millennials: According to Holly Benson of Infosys,[34] "We used to define 'security' as steady, continuous employment with one firm. What we're seeing is that today's youth define 'security' as having a personal skills portfolio that provides them continued employment security across changing business environments and conditions. So, providing employees with robust skills enhancement and development opportunities does provide security as they define it. Learning and development are the new security." What Infosys calls "liquid skills" allow young people to be flexible and adapt quickly to the changing labour market.

Loyalty is no longer to an employer, particularly as, in many cases today, only a few stakeholders share the largest portion of value and distribute whatever remains to the rest of the group. The majority of people consider such an entity to be simply a means or path to getting something they desire – whether benefits, pay, status, promotion, or other end goal. In fact, this perception may be the main problem in many workforce issues that arise.

Wikipedia[35] describes the organisation called "company" as follows, with the last section (in bold) being the most significant:

---

[34] Sarah K. White, CIO, "Millennials in Emerging Markets Express Career Optimism" (February 9, 2016).
[35] https://en.wikipedia.org/wiki/Company

"Company members share a common purpose and unite in order to focus their various talents and organize their collectively available skills or resources to achieve specific, declared goals. Companies take various forms such as:

- Voluntary associations, which may include non-profit organizations

- A group of soldiers

- Business entities with an aim of gaining a profit

- Financial entities and banks

A company or association of persons can be created at law as a legal person so that the company in itself can accept limited liability for civil responsibility and taxation incurred as members perform **(or fail)** to discharge their duty within the publicly declared "birth certificate" or published policy."

It appears that, somehow, perhaps deliberately, the responsibility of some stakeholders with regards to the purpose of the "company" is not part of the definition. In fact, the definition refers to the company as a "legal entity" – in other words, a third party from which we detach ourselves from the moment we establish such organisations.

The Problem with Detachment

In my point of view, from the perspective of an incentive philosophy, this meaning represents absolutely the worst incentive one can provide to protect the interests of all stakeholders. In fact, it sounds as though employees or managers can do anything they desire, with or within the company – as long as it is hidden and undiscovered by those in authority – to exploit whatever pleases them, as long as it remains within the legal limits of wherever the company operates. Does that sound familiar? It does to me.

Experts in diverse fields continually advocate for more accountability by leadership, management, employees, and shareholders. Yet, we refuse to change the definition of the underlying platform from which all parties operate, a point that holds true for most parties involved, be it shareholders, managers, or employees. This archaic concept requires improvement; if the status quo remains as is, we will continue to experience deteriorating returns on all sides. No one is immune. In the end, we will realise the need for responsibility, accountability, and leadership from all stakeholders to achieve not only better results, but the best results we can accomplish together.

Helping people to discover their capabilities, encouraging them to be more aware of themselves and their place in the scheme of things, and empowering them to be more responsible for themselves, while guiding them to reach their dreams, can only serve to benefit all stakeholders. Investors need not worry about this new approach, as it is an excellent use of their funds. After all, investing in businesses that employ optimally compatible, committed, and engaged individuals will only maximise the return on their investments, eliminate needless waste of resources, and increase profit margins: a win-win scenario.

The Need for Technology to Accelerate Self-discovery and Awareness

In light of the prevalent disengagement found in many organisations, technology can be a great facilitator during the process of self-discovery and exploration, accelerating the process significantly. However, technology alone is not yet sufficiently developed to assist us with this process and cannot replace – and should not remove the human element from – the efforts needed for personal reflection or finding one's true path. One hopes an appropriate vehicle may exist in the future, providing stronger tools at our disposal to accelerate the process. For the moment, individuals must use what is available, while seeking and welcoming new improvements and innovations every day.

The most critical factor of technology is deciding what technology to use of the many methods available. All tout themselves to be the "holy grail" of the domain with which they are concerned, though few succeed to the degree they proclaim. Although technology attempts to resolve society's issues through new tools, it cannot provide a lasting solution by offering the same old tools dressed in a shinier package. Radical ideas are necessary, ideas that support a person's actively taking charge and adjusting their own actions with the help of technology. Technology needs to empower people from within, not from without – the changes must come with the help of technology, not made by technology.

For example, some believe that technological solutions should adapt to the way people live today; that is, find an opening to penetrate their thoughts or lives while they are doing what they are doing. What this approach represents is simply, "You can continue doing whatever you are doing today. While you are doing that, we can change things for you." Unfortunately, this concept is charming, and people like charming things. Although attractive, such a concept misses the point, as the following example illustrates.

<u>The Dieting Dilemma:</u> The charming concept may be the reason why many people with weight problems fall in love with seductive promises, despite the fact that the majority of specialised diets (whether or not they have nutritional value), fitness technology gadgets, and calorie-counting gizmos do not work because the product or service they buy has no lasting effects. What happens when dieters stop using the costly, specially prepared meals or find that counting calories or fat grams is too much of a bother (or they lose the shiny bit of technology that tracks their progress – or lack of it)? Often, to the frustration of the dieter, the lost weight finds its way back home.

<u>The Dieting Solution:</u> At the core of the problem, the diets and technological "supports" do not empower their users to change their lifestyle or to reach for deeper knowledge about the true effects of what they are doing to their body by continuing to eat the same way every day. The advertisements, instead, encourage dieters to buy these products and services in perpetuity in order to reach and maintain their desired weight. They do not address the emotional, physical, or

psychological reasons that underlie a dieter's gain/loss cycle and why they react to events in their life as they do. The technology to effectively and successfully address this issue must offer an approach to support self-awareness.

Whatever issue technology is created to resolve (whether dieting, fitness, or other), the lasting impact of any such product or service, after discontinued use, can only come from a deeper acknowledgement and insight that transform your thought process and opinions – which are, incidentally, two very different things. Although your opinions may change over time, if you implement a conscious solid process as to how you perceive and reason in your mind, that process does not change often. However, many people become the victims of their long-established thought process, similar to the concept of self-prophecy. You are, after all, what you believe you are. If your thought process is inefficient and ineffective, thereby derailing you on your most critical decisions (such as your livelihood), then it is imperative to take a good look and try to improve it in order to get back on track.

So, we need to use solutions that offer lasting, long-term benefits. The use of technology in self-discovery and exploration, as well as compatibility between parties, is no exception. Consider this example from an employer's perspective, whereby the company is not going to find its next best talent and optimal candidate by:

- Asking tricky questions through an online survey

- Placing potential candidates into awkward situations to see how they react to a stressful environment in job interviews

- Painting a fake picture of the organisation to deceive candidates by making them believe that the company is a great place to work and they can progress in their careers, when, in fact, recruiters, personally, do not believe what they say

- Encouraging an external hiring process that is based on referrals without following up or checking (in other words, without the technology to manage such processes) how previous hires by that specific referrer might have performed historically

The bottom-line is simple: Management can find the right candidates for the right positions in a timely manner based on technologies that bring transparency to communication, urge authenticity in people, and enable genuine human relationships.

The Opportunity for Emerging Market Economies

When it comes to moving forward, emerging market economies possess tremendous opportunities to accelerate growth and surpass the levels of economic health in developed markets for a number of reasons. Emerging markets:

- Have something that developed markets do not often display: self-motivation.

- Have much younger populations at present.

- Are generally more open to change and willing to attempt new approaches.

Beyond these reasons, the playing field is nearly equal. The proclaimed advantage of low-cost labour is already out-of-date; no nation will win that race because there is no winner in the long run. The quicker that emerging markets realise this fact, the sooner they will start to build economies that are sustainable over time. Price competition at a national level will only result, ultimately, in misery and deception, even though people may experience an uptick in their overall income level.

Although the populations in developed markets are creative and advanced, they generally lack self-motivation. The legislative environment, along with relatively higher costs and risks of failure, prevent potential entrepreneurs, management, and individuals from trying state-of-the-art approaches to increase productivity and sustainability. In many cases, people exit the developed market for emerging market opportunities – or else settle for whatever they possess until retirement. Developed markets may still lead in the number of new patent rights and innovation due to significantly better infrastructure, quality of education (although there is increasing doubt about that recently), and maturity of competitiveness. However, that lead might soon change due to the accelerated progress in some emerging markets, eventually equalising all markets.

The younger generation has a role to play in moving emerging markets forward through their view of the employee-employer relationship. Across developed and emerging markets, according to the 2016

Deloitte Millennial Survey, "millennials feel that most businesses have no ambition beyond profit. ... Millennials often put their personal values ahead of organisational goals." When asked to cite the values that support long-term business success, millennials overall replied:

- Employee satisfaction, loyalty, fair treatment (26%)

- Ethics, trust, integrity, honesty (25%)

- Customer care, focus (19%)

According to the survey, millennials in emerging markets are the least loyal to their current employers. When asked whether they expect to leave their organisation in the next five years, for example, 82% of millennials in Peru agreed, 76% in South Africa and India, 74% in South Korea – compared to 64% in the US and 52% in Japan.

But millennials are not the only segment of the population that bears watching. Retired (or retiring) individuals often represent an unexploited resource in many markets, with few organisations viewing them as being a potential source of growth and innovation. Unfortunately, the term "retirement" does not connote an immediately accessible productive resource, which presents a number of issues:

- A very valuable experience pool of talent is untapped and remains idle until it perishes.

- Viewing something as a cost instead of an asset leads to decisions that are not necessarily value driven.

- Wisdom, a most valued virtue, is not shared and disseminated with the rest of the population as it should be. Consequently, younger generations continue to make avoidable mistakes, triggering further persistent costs to society at large.

But the situation does not have to be this way. We can create a value-oriented generation by facilitating a process and deploying a technology to bridge the experience, knowledge, and wisdom of the retired population with a younger generation who possess authentic inclinations. That untapped value can prove simultaneously beneficial not only to individuals, but also communities, organisations, and nations.

The key opportunity for all markets is to rapidly recognise the potential in all segments of the working population and facilitate the self-discovery process for every citizen. That is the only sustainable growth model that can prevail in the long term. Although it may sound idealistic, today's technology could enable this process even at a national level, helping countries to accelerate growth in all emerging markets.

Technology as a Workable Solution for Individuals, Educators, and Employers

When considering the potential progress and evolution we can experience as a society – with the full use of all generations representing diverse talent in both developed and emerging world markets – the need for technology to enable and support this movement is essential. Technological tools that bridge the gap between organisational strategy and personal desires can provide the necessary impetus toward empowerment, leadership, and self-knowledge.

Consider the situation from the perspective of educators and employers. Faced with increasing expenditures of time and money, which ultimately impact the organisation's bottom line, school administrators and employers need proactive and efficient alternatives. Algorithms, or formulas, that are capable of discovering the right combination of talent and skill amid overwhelming numbers of applicants can change that end result, potentially minimising the risk factors of choosing the wrong major/school or employing the wrong person.

After all, the application process is often a throw of the dice —and the pairing of individual with organisation may very well prove unprofitable and unproductive for either or both parties if not carried out in an objective, rational manner.

One promising solution to the dilemma is sparkChief ™, an innovative diagnostic tool that analyses the background and potential of applicants, offering a genuine spark of hope for students, educators, job seekers, and employers. The algorithm, on which the tool is based, encompasses a set of criteria to examine the underlying current understanding and status of a person's progress towards fulfilling his or her goals. More important, for a minimal fee, the system has the capability to swiftly team up an individual with an organisation, so that students have a clearer view of their future careers and job seekers can receive job offers after inputting their information into the database. Time and money well spent when one considers the wasteful extravagance of the traditional recruiting or admissions process.

Why an Algorithm Works

The science behind the algorithm, called "advanced personal progress scanning" (APPS), separates the core factors that form the foundation of a candidate's career and aspirations. It quantitatively considers the individual's weaknesses, strengths, potentials, strategy, skills, goals, actions, and personal vision – resulting in a user-friendly model built upon the data captured by the software. The tool does not merely match similar words in a person's cv/resume with a company's position description. Instead, it goes beyond a simplistic "search and find" function to analyse the person's experience and potentials. By comparing candidate results to detailed job profiles submitted by employers (or parameters used by educational institutions) in a measurable, rather than subjective, manner, it enhances the ability of the typical administrator to make optimal pairings quickly and inexpensively.

Technology plus human discretion and intelligence may prove to be the solution that is needed today, transforming the application process from a nightmare to a practical reality. In the search for engaged students and key staff, organisations – whether educational, corporations of all sizes, non-profit, government, or nongovernment in different industries and world regions – look for a certain kind of talent, actual experience, and specific skills.

- School administrators seek the right students to match the mission of the facility with the student's course of study and desires. Misalignment can lead to costly transfers, changes in majors, wasted semesters, and increased debt.

- Recruiters attempt to fill vacancies, created by either new jobs or turnover when previous candidates fail to perform. Hiring the wrong person increases recruiting costs (to replace the unsuccessful employee) and training costs (to bring the new employee up to speed). Consequently, if the right candidate is hired (with appropriate skills) the first time and recruiting costs lowered, training costs should be minimal, too, along with other benefits.

The Answer: Human Judgment + Machine Technology

Combining an effective algorithm that works quickly and easily with human discretion and skill can result in positive scenarios, whereby:

- Only qualified candidates are considered, as appropriate individuals find the best job position, resulting in more time spent on the right people.

- Better focus is placed on suitable talent without "settling" for an unqualified candidate, simply to fill the vacancy.

- Application processes work with improved efficiency, bypassing the need to bring in more administrators or recruiting staff (who, in turn, would result in higher employee-related costs for compensation and benefits).

- The application process demonstrates increased objectivity, measurability, reliability, and transparency – resulting in improved credibility to stakeholders.

- Less money is spent on advertisements, agencies, repetitive sign-on bonuses, and so on.

To flourish, organisations depend on finding the right person for the right position in the right place and at the right time. If successful, technology opens the possibility of revolutionising the application process by transforming traditional hiring and career planning into a scientific, efficient, and effective strategy.

- From the individual's perspective, having skills and a high potential without access to the right opportunities is worthless. Such a tool allows talent – often lost in the crowd, unknown and unrecognised – to come to the attention of organisational recruiters. As it helps administrators sift through thousands of candidate applications to find the best person who can make a positive contribution to the organisation, technology simultaneously advances the individual's career.

- From the organisation's perspective, finding the right talent can boost the success rate of the recruiting function, reduce related costs, significantly improve organisational performance through bringing in engaged and motivated individuals, and boost the organisation's long-term viability in an ever-competitive marketplace.

A well-designed diagnostic tool can sort the right candidates from the wrong ones, allowing an organisation to swiftly find the individual who represents the best fit – not merely comes close – to the specifications of the organisation's requirements.

Partnering to Reach the Same Goal

The reasons for using such a tool as sparkChief™ are persuasive, particularly for individuals. However, recruiters might very well balk at implementing such a system, viewing the technology as a threat to their own jobs. It is all about perspective. If the tool could result in better use of organisational dollars, more efficient expenditure of time, and a cadre of qualified candidates, it can prove to be a win-win solution.

The human factor will always be a participant in the application process. The algorithm can only work if (a) candidates provide accurate data and remain true to themselves about their skills, requirements, and desires, and (b) administrators exercise discretion and judgment. As time goes on, more and more organisations will acknowledge the advantages of adding a quantitative method to their subjective processes. Not only is it common sense, but it is also simply a matter of time.

CHAPTER 5:

GETTING READY FOR THE FUTURE: THE ROADMAP

To help individuals address the need for lifelong learning, personal leadership, and self-awareness – and organisations, as well – the algorithm behind the sparkChief™ model incorporates specific criteria. Those factors, accompanied by honest input from the user, serve as a roadmap whereby a person can understand and determine the best fit for one's knowledge, talent, desires, and goals. This information can lead a person toward the right path – be it education, employment, or simply a fulfilling life.

The model considers four general stages of progress to move from thought and ideas to practical action.

1. *The Roadmap: Enlightenment*

Enlightenment conjures up the concepts of insight, awareness, wisdom, education, learning, and knowledge. This stage represents the initial steps that reveal the different aspects of the self – some of which may have been undiscovered and, therefore, untapped. It discusses an individual's values and purpose in life, along with a fair assessment of the abilities that a person can offer.

2. *The Roadmap: Validation*

Validation refers to checking or proving the validity or accuracy of something. This stage affirms the self-knowledge gathered, allowing the user to recognise and think about how one can build on that foundation to look toward a better, more meaningful future in practical terms.

3. *The Roadmap: Synthesising*

Synthesising involves combining a number of things or elements into a coherent whole to make something new and unique. This stage represents an exploration of the external environment, as well as the trends that influence our decisions. It helps us to understand the reality of the world around us and how we can work within the limitations of existing conditions to negotiate a path that will lead toward achievement of our goals.

4. The Roadmap: Execution

Execution, the final stage, refers to the actual carrying out or putting into effect a plan or course of action. With all the pertinent information in place – both internal and external factors – this phase sets achievable objectives that are concrete and reasonable, yet stretches a person's abilities to reach untapped potential. With these objectives in mind, the individual can make informed decisions to take action, placing control of one's life, as much as possible, in one's own hands.

The following case studies present practical examples of how people can benefit from an honest self-assessment through the sparkChief™ tool.

Case Study 1: Caroline – 18-year-old student

The Context and the Issue

Caroline, a high school student, lives in Paris, France. For most of her academic life, she has been an exemplary student with above-average grades and has never failed an exam. Caroline also enjoys a social life with many friends.

Attending her last year of high school, Caroline has difficulty in making up her mind about what she would like to study in college as she works toward earning a bachelor degree. Her journey has been frustrating, so far, especially in the last two years. To make her decision, Caroline tried a number of ways to help her reach a decision, such as talking to her friends, parents, other family members, and teachers – but her efforts have been unsuccessful.

Very concerned about her situation, Caroline does not want to make the wrong choice and regret her decision years later when it might be too late to change her course of study. She needs to resolve the issue soon, with application deadlines fast approaching, in order to choose the right programmes for schools that are in high demand and competitive. Most people whom she has spoken with have told her to listen to her heart and passion, and the rest will follow. However, Carline has never undergone a formal exploration or discovery process to assess the talent of which she is capable of pursuing.

The New Approach

Caroline decides to take the sparkChief Progress Scan to identify and acknowledge the best path for her to follow in terms of deciding on her future studies, as well as a profession as an adult after graduation.

Based on the Progress Scan, which examines 14 critical factors for an individual, Caroline came to a number of realisations. There are a few important factors to which she needs to pay closer attention in order to understand her true path.

- Discovery 1: Although Caroline is a good student and gets along with friends, she has never gone through a thought process to acknowledge what she truly values in life. She recognises that, at her core, she places a high value on helping others and making a difference in their lives.

- Discovery 2: Caroline is convinced that we can find answers to most of our problems in nature. She has a particular interest in exploring how nature reacts to catastrophic outcomes – in other words, the way nature takes its course. She loves being with animals and observing their behaviour and interaction among themselves. Further, Caroline enjoys investigating and learning about subjects of interest with profound detail.

- Discovery 3: Caroline has never thought of exploring these possibilities and articulating how all her ideas can fit together to develop a logical plan to realise her dreams. She was always encouraged to dream, but never guided on how to achieve those desires. To Caroline, things come to life by themselves without any need for deliberate planning. If it must happen, it will happen.

Results

After extensive reflection and rigorous validation, backed by honest feedback from people whom she cares for and respects, Caroline decides to study medicine and become a researcher.

Case Study 2: John – 32-year-old artist

The Context and the Issue

John, a very talented artist painter, lives in Huntsville, Alabama. Painting since he was age 14, John has had several local and national shows. Somewhat successful, he has sold a few of his paintings at every show. He also works at a part-time job "to pay the bills"; after all, living solely on his artwork has always been a challenge.

John's dream is to become a nationally recognised artist painter. Although he believes he is doing everything he should to achieve this goal, he feels as though he is missing something important. That missing element, he believes, would accelerate his efforts and allow him to put the pieces together to expedite his path to success. His parents always tell him that he needs more exposure and perhaps should consider an alternative approach.

The New Approach

John decides to take the sparkChief Progress Scan to discover what factors might be blocking him, as well as acknowledge what else he needs to focus on to reach his ultimate goal and realise his vision.

Based on the Progress Scan, which examines 14 critical factors for an individual, John came to a number of realisations. There are a few important factors to which he needs to pay closer attention in order to accelerate his efforts.

- Discovery 1: John loves the city in which he lives. After all, he was born and raised there and never considered that it might offer fewer opportunities than a major metropolitan city. A larger locale would allow him to meet with more people in the art world, such as collectors, gallery owners, and curators. But John always thought that, being a good artist, someone would discover him some day.

- Discovery 2: John is creative and loves to spend time alone. Therefore, most of the time, he shies away from friendly gatherings, especially when there are people that he does not know well. He never expected this behaviour to block him from progressing in any way. John always felt that if people like his art, then they should just appreciate it and he would become famous.

Results

After extensive reflection and rigorous validation, backed by honest feedback from people whom he cares for and respects, John applies for, and is accepted in, an artist-in-residence program in Los Angeles. After meeting a new partner in the programme, John decides to move to Los Angeles. He soon announces his first major solo show in an upcoming gallery in the city.

Case Study 3: Steve – 30-year-old employee

The Context and the Issue

Steve, who lives in London, UK, started his career right after graduation from the university with an MBA degree. So far, he has been successful and earns a good salary in his second key role as a marketing manager for a multinational consumer goods company. Steve is about to start a new family with his girlfriend, whom he met through friends a couple of years ago. He has always achieved his objectives at work and, at times, even exceeded them. He gets along with his peers, as well as his boss, who describes Steve as a "high-potential" employee.

However, Steve is a bit concerned about his future. Although he enjoys his work, he also believes that he would not like to do the same thing for the rest of his career. According to his mentors, Steve needs to work his way through all the functions, regions, and a few business units to truly progress in his career. Lately, Steve has faced a challenging period as he wonders whether the consumer goods industry is the right sector in which to build a career. In addition, the buzz from his colleagues is that the sector is experiencing pressure to be more efficient and cost-conscious, with margins falling due to ever-increasing competitiveness in the global economy.

Although Steve has had many discussions and exchanges with close friends, his girlfriend, and parents, he senses that those conversations missed something more profound than their tactical suggestions. He feels he needs to go deeper on his own to bring together his ideas and thoughts, together with the advice he has received, in order to determine his next move before navigating further along his career path. After all, he hates the thought of finding himself unhappy and unsatisfied with his career choice at age 45 when it would likely be more challenging to make a change.

The New Approach
Steve decides to take the sparkChief Progress Scan to assess and conceive a plan for his future to enhance his career and develop himself as an individual, while inspiring others.

Based on the Progress Scan, which examines 14 critical factors for an individual, Steve came to a number of realisations. There are a few important factors to which he needs to pay closer attention to discover the most effective approach for him to progress forward.

- Discovery 1: Although Steve seems focused and has had a successful track record so far, he has never given thought to what truly drives him in life. He recognises that, at the bottom of his heart, he cares deeply about learning new things and applying knowledge for the benefit of other people.

- Discovery 2: Steve strong believes that without learning, one cannot be successful in life, especially with all the advancement taking place everywhere due to technology. He discovers that he has a particular interest in communications and how we use it to explain things to each other. Steve has been tinkering with his "pet project" to establish a blog focused solely on how people from different cultures define and use different means of communication to connect with each other. While he loves reading and learning about new subjects, Steve also loves writing. He realises that the reason he wanted to build his blog was to practice all these desires simultaneously.

Results

After extensive reflection and rigorous validation, backed by honest feedback from people whom he really cares for and respects, Steve decides to move into the media sector. He plans to become a content development and purchasing director in a leading publishing house in London.

Case Study 4: Bo – 45-year-old Human Resources executive

The Context and the Issue

Bo works at a leading international logistics firm, based in Singapore. She started her career in HR 20 years ago. While she has worked for many large multinationals, mostly in their regional operations in Asia Pacific, Bo has also lived and worked in New York as an expatriate for three years. She has a very global mindset and is considered to be one of the most influential HR executives in Singapore. During her time in HR, Bo's experience has touched on nearly all aspects of the field, including rewards, talent management, and international assignments. As a well-rounded HR executive, Bo is a frequent speaker at conferences and forums across the region.

Recently, her leadership team gave her a mandate to closely align her company business strategy with their workforce strategy. The leadership team wants Bo to move quickly on this project, encouraging her to be as open-minded as possible in terms of finding new approaches to allow the company to significantly improve its performance vs. that of its competitors. The latest engagement survey findings indicate that a majority of regional employees are satisfied with their leadership team, yet there seems to be a tendency to leave the company if another opportunity appears on their doorstep.

The company bases its current business strategy on a fast-track growth model that necessitates creativity in all functions, departments, and business units. The shareholders want to accelerate earnings and maximise their return on their invested capital. In addition, while market conditions have been deteriorating in some key markets, they are still relatively better than in other regions, considering what has been happening in Europe. The leadership, therefore, believes that the company needs a new approach to organise its business and empower its workforce to perform at an optimum level, thereby placing the company in a leading position among regional competitors.

Bo has been an advocate for change for a long time within the firm. However, as the situation seemed acceptable and margins were achieved, no one in the company dared to rock the boat – particularly in recent years when most sector companies faced turbulent times across the region. Bo is determined not to settle for a short-term solution or follow a traditional strategy that most companies follow – that is, go through a typical reorganisation process, eliminate excess capacity in the workforce, downgrade some roles to reduce workforce costs, load employees with more responsibility, and, ultimately, declare victory because the firm gained a couple of more points on their net operating income.

The New Approach

Bo decides to do something different, convincing the management team to address the root cause of their problems rather than the symptoms. She implements the sparkChief Progress model and scans the entire employee population to obtain a more truthful reading of the organisation. Although her strategy entails a risk, she is willing to take it despite the potential for unpleasant findings (transparent as they are). However, it will allow the firm to undertake a profoundly fresh start to develop and grow its potential and achieve unprecedented higher performance levels.

Based on the Progress Scan, which examines 14 critical factors for each employee, the leadership team came to a number of realisations. There are a few important factors regarding their current organisation that require immediate attention in order for the company to improve margins, ready the firm for accelerated growth, and benefit all stakeholders (shareholders, board members, management, and employees).

- Discovery 1: Bo discovers that almost 70% of employees do not share the company's mission. Although employees seem content with the leadership and perform reasonably according to set objectives, management never asked them if they shared or cared about the mission of the firm set forward by the leadership. The company modified its mission in recent years, but never validated it as to employees' beliefs. Management assumed that the new mission should, by default, be accepted by all employees. The mission statements appear in annual reports, are included on company intranets, and are displayed on corporate office walls. But the simple truth is that by not enlisting employee support, the company caused an unspoken misalignment at the foundational level within the organisation.

- Discovery 2: Bo, as a very seasoned HR professional, strongly believes that investment in training is a good thing, often proving itself worthwhile, and so encourages spending more training dollars on all employees. However, strangely enough, when recent engagement surveys asked why people would leave the firm, most employees responded, "for better career development opportunities." That response did not make sense for a company willing to invest in training to help employees better themselves at their job. Bo discovered that actually providing training to the misaligned employees resulted in a conventionally acceptable return, but never an outstanding outcome for "all employees."

Results

After extensive reflection and rigorous validation, backed by honest feedback from employees who truly shared, cared about, and were committed to the company strategy, the firm decided to only hire employees who love what they do and commit themselves to improve both company results and further their careers. The firm also plans to implement a new programme to transition employees to roles in which they would be more effective.

Case Study 5: Alejandra – 50-year-old teacher

The Context and the Issue

Alejandra, a high school teacher, lives in Mexico City, Mexico. A passionate teacher, she also presides over the student advisory board at her school. Teaching all her adult life, Alejandra often observes frustration in many of her students about their education, as well as their relationships among themselves. Although some students are excellent achievers in their studies, they lack determination and foresight in deciding what to do in their lives.

Alejandra wonders how she could be of help to students to decide whom they want to become. She strongly believes that students lack formal guidance and direction from their parents and teachers about the real world, acknowledging the lack of individualised care provided to students by the academic system. In a way, teachers tell the students to digest the content they receive, testing them on outcomes in terms of their level of absorption. There is no differentiation if a student is interested in or likes a subject. They follow a curriculum dictated by the education ministry, whereby they receive a diploma if they study as instructed.

Some students are fortunate to discover their calling and declare what they want to become after school; however, this self-knowledge is an exception rather than a norm. Alejandra wants to help students decide their futures, not simply earn a diploma at graduation. In her opinion, the end game should not be a piece of paper, but a mindset equipped with the necessary tools to build future citizens, families, communities, careers, and a nation that encourages everyone to discover one's self and progress as an individual in society. Since she leads the student advisory board at her school, Alejandra thinks that students need a new approach to allow each individual to paint his or her own future and put everything in perspective to eventually facilitate personal development.

The New Approach

Alejandra decides to provide the sparkChief Progress Scan to all students age 14 to 18 to obtain a diagnostic in terms of where they stand at a given time and what they need to do achieve their goals.

Based on the Progress Scan, which examines 14 critical factors for each student, Alejandra came to a number of realisations. There are a few important factors to which the students need to pay closer attention in order to explore their potential.

- Discovery 1: Although the majority of students, on average, are good academically, most have never gone through a formal process of thinking or been encouraged to discover what they truly want to do as they become adults. Students feel that they are there to please their teachers and parents with good academic results. Alejandra recognises that most students are not comfortable about articulating their inner desires, often remaining in the dark within their own minds.

- Discovery 2: Alejandra discovers that by asking the right questions, students are empowered to share their authentic thoughts and not shy away from expressing themselves.

Results

After extensive reflection and rigorous validation, backed by honest feedback from teachers that the students care for and respect, along with their parents, Alejandra and the advisory board start using a framework to guide students in making more informed decisions about their future potential.

Following the Roadmap into the Future

Through the sparkChief™ model, individuals can undertake a journey of self-discovery that creates a personal portfolio of knowledge, talent, desires, and goals. With this self-awareness, an individual possesses a solid foundation on which to make major and minor decisions throughout every stage of the life cycle – whether it involves family life, community involvement, education, employment, or simply one's personal dreams. It serves as a vehicle through which an individual can evaluate whether personal goals are a fit for a course of study, career, or an employer's culture.

But to be proactive and move forward in life requires an understanding of a simple and basic truth: There can be no progression without first dealing with the root cause of a problem or condition. People need to take time and dive deep into themselves to explore what is possible and what is feasible – to step beyond a life of complacency and mediocrity to resolve whatever issues they may face. By shining light on the core of our identities – who we are, what we value, and of what we are capable – we are then able to lead a fulfilling life on our own terms.

However, some individuals persist in telling themselves that they are not capable of doing anything – a patently false statement, as everyone is capable of doing at least something. Every individual has a talent, a reason to be. The likelihood is that most people just do not know what that may be or perhaps lack support in discovering what it can be. Unfortunately, such people remain in the dark – sometimes for a long time, and, sadly, sometimes until the end of their lives.

This reservoir of untapped potential represents a significant waste. One should not doubt, but should, instead, seek guidance to fulfil one's capability and make a positive contribution to the world in which one lives.

CHAPTER 6:

PRACTICAL STRATEGIES FOR FOLLOWING THE ROADMAP

The factors included in the sparkChief™ model lead an individual through a step-by-step examination of what lies at the core of a person's purpose in life. Through the stages of enlightenment, validation, synthesising, and execution, the user reaches a place that points toward a path filled with potential opportunity.

But the process requires a cautious approach for optimal results. The following discussion provides practical suggestions about what a person should expect when navigating through the sparkChief™ roadmap – or any other self-assessment tool.

Seven Key Points for Following the Roadmap

1. Timing is, as always, important.

When faced with a major life decision, step back, take a deep breath, and consider all options before taking action. The choices involved at different stages can be overwhelming – finding a passion, choosing a course of study, advancing in a career, finding a life mate to start a family, starting a business, re-inventing oneself, thinking about volunteer efforts, and so on. At times, the decisions that one is pressured to make can coincide; for example, finding a life partner and seeking a new job. While the issues may differ, the end point is the same: find the best person or position or whatever that best suits your needs and desires.

2. Verify your core values thoroughly.

Possibly one of the most important criteria, one's core values lay the foundation for major life decisions. These choices can have a significant impact on a person's family, peer group, and others. Reflecting on core personal values should take as much time and effort as necessary to understand what makes you tick.

When doing so, consider whether the values you have stated are the ones in which you truly believe – or, whether they are values you are expected to uphold, as suggested by family members, peers, an employer or mentor, or society at large. The values should be a reflection of a genuine "you." Honesty, here, is essential.

3. *Seek out objective feedback, even from people you do not appreciate.*

When conducting a self-assessment, it is helpful to ask mentors for their suggestions and feedback, but take your own advice. After all, who knows you better than you do?

Mentors at different life stages – not only during a period of introspection – offer value if the relationship is based on true, independent, and authentic communication. Remember, mentors should be there to provide you with objective commentary. Although some feedback may not be positive, it should be constructive. If the mentorship is based on mutual interests, thereby lacking objectivity and honesty, then you are not talking to the right people.

Mentors are not the only source of guidance. People who "like" you, who share mutual respect and affection, are likely to offer positive feedback only. Those whom you may not appreciate – or get along with – may have a very different view of you, possibly one that is not 100% favorable. Recognising how they think about you, even though you do not agree with their perspective or opinions, can offer a decided advantage that may prompt you to reconsider your views on who you really are. It may prompt you to accept something negative about yourself that you may have been avoiding, thereby offering improvement and growth.

But remember, a different perspective is just another perspective, that's all. Acknowledgement does not mean acceptance. Once more, be honest.

4. *Take time to reflect. Do not rush to conclusions and follow the steps – don't skip!*

Unfortunately, the world we live in is all about shortcuts and instant gratification. Everyone seeks a shortcut to something, an easy way to achieve what we want without putting too much time and effort into it. But to become a mature individual and sustain fulfilment, it is far better to reach that goal through gaining a full awareness and authentic acceptance of whom you are – not the person whom a quick test assumes you to be. That is the only way to grow as a person.

Learning about oneself is not a process that should be rushed. When discovering different aspects about yourself that may have gone unrecognised and hidden – or, possibly, avoided – take time to think about the implications for your life and reflect on the possibilities they open up.

There is no off-the-shelf miraculous solution waiting at the end of the process. The roadmap works in two ways, by providing:

- A quick snapshot of where you are at this point in your life, and
- A mindset to explore your path to fulfilment.

The first point is a quick exercise, while the second one will involve time and effort to finalise. If you attempt to rush to conclusions about what you discover, without taking your time to think and reflect about each new finding (because you assume you already covered that criteria), you run the risk of bypassing the opportunity to make strategic, informed decisions. Doing so haphazardly will either cause you to waste time or misguide your direction.

5. *Sleep on it, but don't wait too long.*

Once you have gone through everything that the process of self-discovery entails, sleep on your reflections. Some thoughts change when the conscious mind stays away from them for a while; some do not. Stick with the ones that remain the same after careful reflection.

Although a person should not rush through the self-discovery journey, don't wait too long either. The quicker you start acknowledging the facts and making concrete plans to change or improve your life, the better your chances of achieving whatever you desire. Timing, as they say, is everything.

6. *Walk your talk and act accordingly.*

Thoughts without action are meaningless pipedreams. Once you complete the self-analysis, take steps to ensure that every resource at your disposal is geared toward meeting those objectives in the best way possible.

Focus on your path, and avoid doing anything else that will waylay you – but be sure that your actions cause no harm. Navigate your way through life decisions with actions that serve to support your values.

7. Don't limit yourself – revisit your interests.

Sometimes people hesitate about which path to choose to reach their destination, forgetting that there are often many roads available. And, more important, those alternatives are likely to change as time goes on and new opportunities beckon. The only criterion that you should keep in the forefront of your thoughts is that whatever you choose to do should move you in the direction of your goals. Don't follow byways that veer off 10 degrees left or right. Keep your eyes glued to the end point.

That said, from time to time, revisit your initial interests to make sure that you still enjoy doing things that feel right for you. As time progresses, and you pass through different stages of the life cycle, so may your desires and goals change. Stay attuned to your true self and listen to your instincts if they signal a bend in the road.

CHAPTER 7:

PRACTICAL EXAMPLES OF SELF-ASSESSMENT USERS

Self-assessment is not restricted to personal use. Beyond an individual's need to gain self-knowledge, the value of the process lies in its usefulness for people at different stages of their life – whether young students, employees, or job seekers. Further, an assessment offers organisations a practical and effective tool to boost their growth and financial viability through seeking and hiring the right individuals who can bring engagement, talent, expertise, and potential to support the company's strategic vision.

The following examples highlight the ways in which different categories of users can take advantage of a self-assessment process, for example, through the sparkChief™ application.

Users: Students, Teachers, Counsellors, Educators

The ideal way to deploy the proposed self-assessment tool in educational facilities is through the support of students' counsellors. There are two components to the assessment process:

- A quick insight about where each student stands against his or her personal development progress, which is facilitated through a mobile application that provides students with instant feedback on four key dimensions of their personal progress.

- A set of interviews to guide students in their efforts to further explore areas where they feel they need more clarification and validation. Depending on the overall status of each student's personal progress, counsellors need approximately two to three hours to support each student.

Once the validation phase is accomplished, counsellors then guide each student to collate the pieces through interviews and personal reflection time. The outcome of this phase, in terms of time for the student, can vary from a few weeks to a few months, depending on the engagement level of each student, time spent for personal exploration, and feedback from others.

The final step involves making an action plan for each student. Most often, students take the lead during this phase with periodic checks and meetings with counsellors.

The ideal timing to start using the assessment tool is two years prior to graduation from high school. However, a student can also use the tool during the last year of high school – or even beyond graduation.

Users: Job Seekers (Employees Seeking New Opportunities, Untapped/Unemployed Persons)

The ideal way to deploy the proposed self-assessment tool for individuals seeking work is through the assistance of personal coaches. There are two components to the assessment process:

- A quick insight about where each employee/unemployed person stands against his or her personal development progress, which is facilitated through a mobile application that provides them with instant feedback on four key dimensions of their personal progress.

- A set of interviews to guide employees/unemployed persons in their efforts to further explore areas where they feel they need more clarification and validation; depending on the overall status of each individual's personal progress, coaches need approximately two to four hours to support each individual.

Once the validation phase is accomplished, personal coaches then guide each employee/unemployed person to collate the pieces through interviews and personal reflection time. The outcome of this phase, in terms of time for the individual, can vary from a few weeks to a few months, depending on the engagement level of each individual, time spent for personal exploration, and feedback from others. The overall time needed with a coach during this phase can be somewhere between two and three hours.

The final step involves making an action plan for each employee/unemployed person. Most often, individuals take the lead during this phase with periodic checks and meetings with personal coaches.

Any current employee, job seeker, or untapped person (a.k.a. unemployed)[36] can use the assessment tool at any time in their career to assess and explore their potential or confirm the direction they have taken earlier in their career.

Users: Employers

The ideal way to deploy the proposed self-assessment tool in organisations is through the assistance of independent consultants. There are two components to the assessment process:

- A summary report about where the total employee population stands against company vision, objectives, and business strategy at a given time, which is facilitated through an aggregate analysis of employees' assessment results based on four key dimensions of their profile.

---

[36] See conclusion for a specific discussion of unemployed individuals.

- A set of executive meetings to guide management in their efforts to further explore areas of compatibility between business goals and workforce needs, followed by discussions to further clarify or validate goals if necessary. Depending on the overall gaps uncovered, these meetings need approximately two to three hours to guide the management team.

Once the validation phase is accomplished, independent consultants then guide the management team to bring the pieces together through a series of senior-level interviews. The outcome of this phase, in terms of time for the individual, can vary from a few weeks to few months, depending on the engagement level of the leadership team and support from management. The overall time needed with senior leadership during this phase is somewhere between two to three hours.

The final step involves making an action plan for the organisation. Most often, leadership drives this phase with regular meetings with independent consultants.

Employers can deploy the assessment tool at any time in their organisations to assess and diagnose the gaps between business goals and workforce needs to accelerate significant growth or to confirm its strategic direction taken earlier.

Users: Recruiters

The ideal way to deploy the proposed self-assessment tool is with job applicants. There are two components to the assessment process:

- A quick scan about where each applicant stands against his or her personal development progress as an individual, which is facilitated through a mobile application that provides applicants with instant feedback on four key dimensions of their personal progress.

- A plot of applicant results against the recruiter's job profile criteria based on organisational requirements. Only applicants, based on the recruiter's definition, corresponding to the company and job profile, go forward to the next phase of the recruitment process.

Once the filtering process is accomplished, each applicant moves on to interviews and the validation period. The outcome of this phase, in terms of time for the applicant, can vary from a few weeks to a few months, depending on the flow of the hiring process by the recruiter. However, the overall time needed throughout the recruitment cycle drastically reduces as recruiters only focus on candidates with the highest compatibility.

The final step involves making an action plan to decide on the appropriate applicant and make the individual a job offer.

Any applicant can undergo an assessment at any time during the application process to determine the individual's potential and compatibility with the organisation.

Users: Human Resources During Reorganisation/Separation

The ideal way to deploy the proposed self-assessment tool is during any reorganisation effort. There are two components to the assessment process:

- A quick scan about where each member of a business line or function stands against his or her personal development progress as an individual, which is facilitated through a mobile application that provides individuals with instant feedback on four key dimensions of their personal progress.

- A plot of each employee in each business unit or function against the company's new organisation profile based on new business requirements. Only employees corresponding to new job profiles, based on the newly designed organisation structure, are eligible for positions within the business unit or function.

Once the streamlining process is accomplished, employees who remain move on to validation through interviews. The outcome of this phase, in terms of time for the employee, can vary from a few weeks to a few months, depending on the flow of the reorganisation efforts. However, the overall time needed throughout the reorganisation cycle drastically reduces as the leadership team only focuses on employees that indicate the highest compatibility.

Although all employees within the concerned business unit or function undergo the same assessment process, the results assess a percentage of employees who are not compatible with the new organisational strategy. HR personnel guide those individuals to move on to more compatible units or functions within the company, if possible. If there is no appropriate position within the company, independent coaches guide these employees toward the next steps to find opportunities outside the firm through additional interviews and personal reflection time.

The outcome of this phase, in terms of time for the employee, can vary from a few weeks to a few months, depending on the engagement level of each employee, time spent for personal exploration, and feedback from others. The overall time needed with a coach during this phase is somewhere between four and six hours.

Any employee can undergo assessment at any time during the reorganisation/separation process to determine the individual's potential and compatibility with the organisation.

Suggestions for Users in Obtaining Feedback During Self-Assessment

No matter the category – whether the user is an individual seeking self-knowledge or an organisation conducting an employee survey – the process of obtaining feedback becomes critical when conducting an honest self-assessment. Although we often wonder how others perceive us in our relations and interactions with them, we seldom ask for their honest feedback and opinions. Good family members, friends, and possibly colleagues might offer honest feedback from time to time. Parents usually do – without being asked!

When considering what people say about us – as individuals or entities – we might dismiss some comments. This reaction may occur, whether or not there is a bit of truth in the feedback we receive from those people who care about us. If those we query are honest, and truly care, it is important to listen to what they say, view it with integrity and an open mind, and decide whether or not it holds true for us. Obtaining such feedback is an essential factor in undergoing such a personal self-learning exercise.

Although the main purpose of feedback is validation, remember that you do not need validation from others – even persons to whom you are close – in order to know or decide what actions you should take in your life. That said, validation serves an important role in determining whether others have a drastically different view of oneself. Should that happen, at the very least, just acknowledging the difference is worthwhile. Without that awareness, a person can run the risk of self-prophecy, as many individuals do, believing things about themselves that are not true. Consider all the people you know who hold on to an image of themselves from, say childhood, an image that their parents imposed upon them – an image, in fact, that they have outgrown or have never really possessed.

When requesting feedback from others, always give them sufficient time to think, reflect, digest, and provide honest feedback. A week is an ideal period. Remind them not to take shortcuts in their responses, as half-baked feedback is worse than no feedback at all. Quick answers might derail you and waste your time. So, if they do not have time or the ability to focus on the process and offer thoughtful feedback, it is preferable to ask someone else.

Self-Assessment: A Matter of Privacy

Remember, as self-assessment is a private matter, a third party without any self-interest in the process is the best entity to sponsor and conduct the analysis. The results from the self-assessment should also be mobile. After all, you own the information and should oversee and possess that data.

If your employer, for example, offers the opportunity to conduct a self-assessment, make sure that you decide what parts to disclose to the employer, based on your self-assessment. The only information your employer needs to know about you is whether your individual profile fits with their business profile. That's all!

CONCLUSION AND FUTURE THOUGHTS

The messages conveyed in this book are not secrets, as every area touched here has been deeply explored. Limitless amounts of literature are available on each subject, as scholars and experts have investigated, researched, and written meticulously about each of these important topics. With all that said, there are yet some thoughts I wish to share.

The Need to Synthesise

The key message I want to convey is that to achieve empowerment and self-awareness, you need to go through a process to synthesise your values, thoughts, capabilities, and knowledge – and coordinate your actions with a deliberate vision. This point is true not only for individuals, but also for families, communities, organisations, societies, and nations.

Although many people I have met over the years often possess all the ingredients necessary to live a more fulfilling life or to be more successful in their efforts to achieve their desired goals, most of them do not take the time to synthesise. Perhaps the problem is that synthesising requires a more creative mind, a more open mind that allows one to explore endlessly – a somewhat difficult task for many people. Of course, we all experience tribal (including family), cultural, societal, traditional, conventional, and religious influences on our lives and decisions. However, this undeniable truth does not have to haunt us throughout our lifetime, especially as it is becoming more difficult to focus on what is important for ourselves due to all the distractions in our day-to-day living.

Part of the difficulty – and maybe it is the worst problem – lies in the misguided advice we receive from seemingly successful people. Such individuals promise that if you, for example, "just follow your passion, you can achieve whatever you wish in life" or "just persist, do not give up, and keep trying (no matter how many times), because in the end you get what you want." Conventional advice – "don't give up", or "you'll meet the right people at the right time who can open doors for you" or "you just need luck" – is not new. Nor is it all wrong.

But the trouble with such advice is that it is unwise if absorbed alone; success and empowerment do not happen in isolation. Synthesis is necessary, one way or another, which is why so many people unintentionally misguide others through simplistic and positive advice. As a result, this type of advice can cause a significant delay in discovering one's capabilities or may actually block people from reaching their own truth.

What if, for example, you were persistent and tried over and over again, hoping to achieve something, but you picked the wrong means and tried endlessly? This cyclical effort is, essentially, the definition as being crazy: trying the same thing over and over and hoping that something different will happen one day. You can – and should – follow your passion and live a fulfilling life; but you cannot only follow your passion and expect to become successful. Every one of us needs to understand the difference between fulfilment and success, because the opposite is also true: You can become successful but not live a fulfilling life.

Many people suffer from this syndrome and live unhappy lives. It is a burning issue today. If we can, one way or another, start helping such individuals to ease their pain and empower them to obtain a more compassionate perspective in life, it can only serve to benefit them, as well as their families, communities, organisations, and nations.

The Need for Transparency

There has been a movement toward transparency since the beginning of the technological advancement in every field. In my point of view, this movement represents the biggest revolution of all. Although technology will continue to bring more openness and transparency in our lives, communities, societies, corporations, and nations, the result may not be something that everyone desires. But we need to empower transparency for ourselves and as a member of society. If we are genuinely honest with ourselves, we can reach our own truths faster.

In the end, transparency will serve all stakeholders, including organisations as a whole; the more they become transparent, the better and more effectively they will serve their shareholders, customers, and workforce. Unfortunately, all stakeholders do not empower, or believe in, this movement, with the opposite true in many organisations. For example, shareholders are not transparent with management, management is not transparent with employees, and employees are not transparent with management – yet alone with themselves. This non-transparency triggers huge hidden costs from wasted resources, finances, and time for all stakeholders – expenditures that many leadership teams might not be able to evaluate or recognise. But hidden or not, this cost in one that all of society continues to pay.

The Need to Invest in Self-Discovery

As corporations continue to invest heavily in training their workforce, many miss a critical point in this endeavour by not investing in the individual employee. The result is a lost opportunity whereby they could be the recipient of a significantly more positive outcome. Organisations today should focus on investing in programmes that facilitate the self-discovery process for their employees to achieve truly sustainable growth and better resource allocation. Although everyone complains about scarce resources, few are interested in transformative change that harvests true engagement and commitment for all stakeholders.

It is common sense. The more self-aware and empowered employees feel, they (and their employers) more they can develop significantly better individual performance, as well as organisational results. Without employees' self-knowledge, corporations will continue to waste and miss opportunities for the foreseeable future.

The Need to Uncover Potential: Unemployed vs. Untapped

The term that defines the population who do not hold a job – "unemployed" – is very misguided, most likely coined originally by people with an archaic vision of modern economy and society (and, perhaps, explain why there has not been a newer version). As defined in Investopedia,[37] "unemployment is a phenomenon that occurs when a person who is actively searching for employment is unable to find work. Unemployment is often used as a measure of the health of the economy. The most frequently measure of unemployment is the unemployment rate, which is the number of unemployed people divided by the number of people in the labour force."

This explanation is, by far, the least insightful definition of unemployment, solely based on a single-minded and irresponsible view of the condition. The majority of people who fall into this category are totally capable individuals with their own convictions, passions, values, and meanings of life. It is just that the organisations (people) that employed them earlier did not know how to extract, or were not at all interested in extracting, the potential of these individuals.

---

[37] http://www.investopedia.com/terms/u/unemployment.asp

The true term should be "untapped" rather than "unemployed" people. Organisations (people) that are unable or incompetent to tap into the potential of their workforce should be fined (or, perhaps, taxed) or left unemployed until they learn otherwise. If not, we will continue to pay the cost for the very few who either remain ignorant or purposefully exploit society at large.

The Need to Choose

Margaret Lobenstine's book[38] deals with the dilemma of wanting to follow multiple passions rather than confining oneself to only one. She contemplates that the people with this characteristic have "Renaissance Souls," which is a more positive attribute of people who might consider themselves to be confused. Wanting to do many things or be as many persons as one might desire is not a problem. It just might require much more energy, ambition, and will power.

With the majority of people struggling to just find a single passion, I think her real message is that you do not need to limit yourself with one interest. But in the end, you still need to choose and focus on the area in which you shine most brightly. If your passions are multiple, stick with them. But make a choice so you do not go through the rest of your life wondering if you took the right path.

---

[38] Margaret Lobenstine, The Renaissance Soul: Life Design for People with Too Many Passions to Pick Just One (The Experiment, 2013).

The Need to Ask the Right Questions

Being able to focus on whatever you do is probably one of the most critical, but underestimated and undervalued, aptitudes in many people's lives. It is not an easy skill to possess, as it requires discipline and practice. To paint a complete picture of ourselves, we must focus on the right things – be it at a personal or organisational level – by asking the right questions. The wrong questions will only waste time as you attempt to find the irrelevant answers to your challenges, which is one reason why some people or businesses struggle with their core.

Asking the right questions requires deep contextual understanding of what is it that you are trying to do – again, whether at the personal or organisational level – which may be why many organisations (people) are frequently tempted to answer only familiar questions. For example, when companies face with what I call the "efficiency disease" – a chronic inflammatory condition caused by forced price competition while constantly trying to find savings without the deep insights of the overall well-being of the organisation and all its stakeholders – they tend to focus on the easiest way out: cutting tangible costs. This short-term solution can, and often does, result in a much deeper pain afterwards.

As Dr. John McDougal[39] states, "people love to hear good news about their bad habits." They easily postpone unfelt pain through quick fixes of relief today, not caring about their future state. When challenged by

---

[39] https://www.drmcdougall.com

potential future conditions, they dismiss compassion for the love of today's pleasure. It is this inability that needs to be developed and progressed, so we can improve the condition and well-being of individuals, families, communities, organisations, nations, and the environment.

The Need to Act

The joke about the person who hopes to win the lotto without actually playing a game has the expected moral of the story: You need to act if you want something to happen. I have met people in all corners of the world and organisation who share the same thought as in the joke, passing the expectation of action to someone else. They say they are not accountable for taking action, which requires energy and compassion, at the very least, for oneself.

But without action, one's life may not move forward. To begin, the first ingredient for action is compassion. To have compassion for oneself (and others, if you are a bit more progressive), you need to prepare the groundwork, which begins within the family. If you are fortunate enough to have compassion very early in life, thanks to your family environment, taking action might be much easier. However, not all of us are lucky, growing up in very diverse family scenarios, which delays our capacity for compassion. We also cannot expect everyone to be compassionate; if that were true, our world would be a much different and more advanced place.

The need to act to change things for the better and improve the lives of millions who are stuck in ignorance, or transform the minds of people who purposefully force others to remain in ignorance, is probably the most important mission we all must embark on. That need starts with each and every one of us.

The Need for –and Phenomenon – of Luck

Luck or randomness is a truth we have difficulty in understanding. Like it or not, luck is a fact, but also a rare phenomenon. Wishing to be lucky is hardwired in many minds. After all, who does not want to be lucky? Further, when we do not know how to explain something, we call it a luck: "That person just got lucky." True to its inherent nature, one can get lucky without any apparent reason.

Dr. Richard Wiseman's book[40] defines luck in terms of increasing one's own probabilities purposefully. He argues that the more opportunities you create for yourself purposefully, the more chances you have to achieve whatever you desire (of course, given the fact that you do all the others things right). In other words, the more you increase your chances of reaching some goal, the luckier you may become. I think this concept is as close as it gets. And it is good advice.

However, we must be careful not to believe that luck is correlated. At its best, luck is random. No one controls their own luck; it is very

---

[40] Dr. Richard Wiseman, The Luck Factor: The Four Essential Principles (Talk Books, 2003).

difficult to correlate luck with either success or failure. So, there is no point in waiting for your own lucky moment. It just happens.

The Last Word

The importance of self-discovery and awareness will become even more critical in our efforts to build better families and communities, more efficient and effective organisations, and more progressive nations. We need transformative change in today's organisations, and the true source of that transformation is the people who make up the organisation.

The journey to realise that vision starts now. One person at a time.

REFERENCES

Gallup

Georgetown University Center on Education and the Workforce

Marketdata Enterprises

National Survey of Student Engagement

Organisation of Economic Cooperation and Development

Penn State Division of Undergraduate Studies

Sustainable Development Solutions Network

The College Board

Trainingindustry.com

US Census Bureau

US Department of Education

US News and World Report

WorkplaceTrends.com

INDEX

Barriers to success	Chapter 3
Education	
And job preparedness	Chapter 1
As percentage of GDP	Chapter 1
Cost of college	Chapter 2
High impact practices	Chapter 1
Training expenditures	Chapter 1
Emerging markets	
Millennials	Chapter 4
Opportunities	Chapter 4
Retirees	Chapter 4
Employees	
Disengagement	Chapters 1, 3
Graduate unemployment	Chapter 2
Meaning of "organisation"	Chapter 4
Mis-hire costs	Chapter 2
Recruiting costs	Chapter 2
Goals, personal vs. organisational	Chapter 1
Happiness	
Maslow's hierarchy	Chapter 3
Well-being statistics	Chapter 3
Leadership	
Global workforce	Chapter 1
Millennials	Chapter 1
sparkChief™	
Advanced personal progress scan	Chapter 4
Case studies	Chapter 5
Practical strategies	Chapter 6
Self-assessment users	Chapter 7
Stages	Chapter 5
Technology as a solution	Chapter 4

www.ingramcontent.com/pod-product-compliance
Lightning Source LLC
Chambersburg PA
CBHW030818180526
45163CB00003B/1337